Basketball's Stunting Defenses

Every man who knows how to read has it in his power to magnify himself, to multiply the ways in which he exists, to make his life full, significant, and interesting.

—ALDOUS HUXLEY

Basketball's Stunting Defenses

Wayne Dobbs
Director of Athletics
Brewton-Parker College

Garland F. Pinholster
Director of Athletics
Oglethorpe University

Englewood Cliffs, N.J.
PRENTICE-HALL, INC.

PRINTED IN THE UNITED STATES OF AMERICA

07247-BC

In Memory of
L. "Pop" Crow, Educator
and
Thurman Ronald Couch, U.S. Marine Corps.

Men who gave their maximum in
service to others.

Foreword

As inevitably as death, taxes, and Sonny Liston's right, I'll receive at least a dozen basketball articles every year that will tap off in this fashion: "The astronomical scores in modern basketball reflect the deteriorating quality of defense. There are few coaches who won't give you the easy basket if they think they can get back two. Being so heavily offense-conscious, they spend little or no time on defense. That's why it is becoming a vanishing art. At Great Garde High, however, defense is accentuated greatly. . . ."

Don't get me wrong. I'm 100% on the side of the defensive purists who preach tough defense, realizing it is a more constant factor of winning than offense. They are absolutely right in their thinking, except for one thing: They do not understand that their philosophy is broadly accepted; that practically every coach is aware of the importance of defense and works like a beaver at it.

Those whopping scores are not the products of poor defense, but of the phenomenal improvement in shooting, dribbling, individual weapons, and fire-engine running. How in the world do you defense the tall, fast, agile jump shooter, the incredibly deceptive drivers, the big powerhouses like Elgin Baylor, Oscar Robertson, Wilt Chamberlain, et al? The simple truth is that there is no foolproof defense against these talented towers. The best you can do is arm your boys with the soundest possible defensive tools—both individual and team.

Make no mistake about it: Defense is not as good as it was 10, 15, or 20 years ago. It's *better*—because it has to be. Never in the history of the game is so much high-powered cerebration being poured into defense. All sorts of deceitful weapons are

constantly being forged to combat the H-bomb offensive mis-
siles. Who, a couple of decades ago, ever heard of a box-and-one, a
diamond-and-two, a triangle-and-two, a three-quarter court press
with man-to-man principles, or all the other tricky defensive variations with which coaches are driving each other nuts these days?

Although all coaches are doing their defensive exercises, let's
face it: some work a lot harder and better at it. Way up in the
defensive hierarchy are Garland F. Pinholster and Wayne
Dobbs. At Oglethorpe University, Coach Pinholster has firmly
established himself as one of the cleverest and most versatile
defensive architects in basketball. A masterful fundamentalist
and an inventive genius, he equips his team with every stratagem
in the book; and when you beat his defense—which takes con-
siderable doing—you are beating the best.

Coach Dobbs is cut out of the same cloth. A former defensive
ace at Oglethorpe, Dobbs is now building his own reputation
as a defensive mastermind. Thanks mostly to defense, he compiled an outstanding record in high school ball and is now re-
constructing the basketball fortunes at Brewton-Parker College.

Master and protégé have pooled their talents wonderfully in
this book. Any coach looking for a little defensive help will
find positively everything he needs in *Basketball's Stunting
Defenses,* which offers a mint of practical, time-tested information on every neoteric facet of the art (and science) of defense. It
expounds more than *17 defensive variations* and, just as important, tells you precisely *when* to use them and *how* to coach them.

The clarity and detail of both the text and the diagrams are
superb, and I doubt whether there is a coach in America (or
Outer Mongolia) who can turn to any section without finding
something he can profitably adopt. *Basketball's Stunting Defenses* is clearly a distinguished contribution to the literature
on basketball coaching.

Herman L. Masin
Editor, *Scholastic Coach*

Preface

    Basketball's Stunting Defenses presents over eighteen different defenses to combat any situation that confronts a coach in his effort to build a winning team. Defensive basketball has moved into a new era with coaches stunting their defenses to surprise their opponents. First-class squads are developing a fundamental defensive approach, then varying their attack as the game situation demands.

    Defense need not be a dull, uninteresting chore any longer. Stunting defenses enable the coach to make defense interesting and meaningful. Every coach is looking for newer and better ways to motivate his boys to greater defensive achievements. Stunting is one approach that has been successful.

    Tips on scouting and teaching stunting defenses are also included in this book. Complete preparation is necessary to implement *any* defense. Defensive teaching aids are also included as a part of the overall approach to defense. These and other ideas will help you to build team morale and instill defensive confidence in each player.

    Repetition through various types of drills teaches the players to perform defensive skills more automatically and naturally. Through these drills, the coach can predict more accurately a player's attitude toward hard work, his ability, coordination and willingness to be coached.

    The defenses described are those which the authors have been in contact with as a player or coach or through conversation with other coaches and observation of the game.

Wayne Dobbs

Acknowledgments

The authors are indebted to many people. To name each person whose ideas have influenced this book would be impossible. Friends and colleagues have contributed in immeasurable ways.

Grateful acknowledgment is extended to the following: Mrs. Evelyn Bosher, typist; Coach Billy Carter, Oglethorpe University; Coach Johnny Guthrie, Coach Tommy Neal and Coach James Estes, Southwest Dekalb High School Coaching staff; Coach Pat Stephens, Druid Hills High School, Herman Masin, Editor, *Scholastic Coach;* and to the players at Southwest Dekalb and Oglethorpe through whose efforts defense has become a symbol of success.

Contents

1

Why Use Stunting Defenses

Basketball has experienced a new trend in recent years that poses a great challenge to coaches everywhere. This trend—stunting defenses—has been responsible for a number of upsets in the basketball world, and apparently it will linger to become a part of every basketball coach's repertoire of defensive tricks. The trend has been referred to by some of the game's keenest strategists as the "defensive revolution." The end results are not yet in sight. Not only does it offer a tremendous challenge offensively for coaches, but it also presents an unparalleled defensive challenge to the ingenuity and teaching ability of the basketball coach.

The variety of defenses that will be described by the authors has been labeled "stunting defenses," because of their variation from the normal type of defenses that have been successfully used by the majority of coaches in years past. Most coaches stress simplicity when teaching defense, and stunting defenses can play an important role in your team's success without any complicating or confusing schemes.

The trend toward stunting defenses had its conception when the zone defense began to play a more prominent role in defensive basketball. Soon it became practical to peg a particular team as a "man-for-man team" or a "zone team." Much to the dismay of opposing coaches, these teams began to employ different defenses during the course of the season. Special preparation was given to teams using more than one defense. Eventually, teams started combining and alternating defenses in the same game. As a result, the stunting defenses arose, which combine the best maneuvers from the zone and man-for-man defenses. Basketball has, in addition, experienced the advent of the so-called giant killers, who have been able to knock off teams with far superior strength.

Just as the jump shot has done much to revolutionize basketball, stunting defenses have contributed to the fast and exciting game being played today. Because there have been few multipurpose offenses—offenses that can be used against man-for-man and zone defenses or a combination of both—teams are no longer content to allow the defense to set up before beginning their offensive attack. They try to move the ball down the floor rapidly, so that defense cannot stunt in order to halt the offensive attack. The result has been the fast-break or a racehorse brand of basketball. The deliberate control type game has been abandoned in many instances because of the failure to cope successfully with stunting defenses.

Coaches who stunt their defenses generally agree on the disadvantages and advantages of employing such tactics. We have found stunting defenses to be most effective when there is a need to:

1. Surprise or confuse the opponents.
2. Change the rhythm of the game.

3. Concentrate the defense on a specific offensive strength of the opponent.

4. Cover up a particular defensive weakness.

5. Give the players a psychological boost by doing something different.

These are some of the advantages that can be utilized by every coach, regardless of the caliber of opposition. Not only will you gain unexpected victories, but you will also attain an inner sense of satisfaction by having done something a "little extra."

SURPRISING OR CONFUSING THE OPPONENTS

Every coach looks for something with which to catch his opponents off-guard. The element of surprise has long been used as an equalizer by coaches when their teams have been pitted against teams of superior strength. Changes in the offensive style of play for the "big game" often result in stirring upsets. Stunting defenses will allow more versatility and greater flexibility to your defensive approach. It keeps the offense thinking; opposing teams never know what to expect. They cannot afford to spend preparatory practices concentrating their offensive work against one defense. They must be prepared to meet anything. Stunting defenses can be important weapons in your defensive arsenal.

Once play is underway, stunting defenses tend to confuse opponents, thus contributing to a lack of confidence that could spoil their over-all play. The offensive players will be faced with a different situation than the one they practiced for. Offensive maneuvers—cutting, screening, passing, etc.—will be more difficult to execute and the effectiveness of the offense will be considerably impaired.

CHANGING THE RHYTHM OF THE GAME

Every team will encounter opponents whose style of play will not blend with theirs. The use of stunting defenses makes an important contribution to over-all game strategy, because these defenses can be used to slow down fast-breaking teams or to force teams that use a conservative pattern brand of basketball to play a more wide open game. Destroying an opposing team's offensive tempo increases your chances of victory.

Coaches have found it easier to stunt their defense against teams incorporating set play systems and patterns as a part of their offense. However, "stunting defenses" have been used successfully against fast-break teams, particularly those teams whose release-out passes and methods of penetrating the defense follow a routine pattern. Pattern teams, when confronted by combination or alternating defenses, usually try to move the ball down the floor faster, in an attempt to score before the defense can get set. If a deliberate, pattern team has not spent many hours (many pattern teams do not practice the offensive fast-break) practicing the fast-break, then bad passes, fumbles, lost balls, and violations will be the expected results of their efforts. Make your opponents play your game. Stunting defenses can be instrumental in helping you accomplish this objective. Remember, the degree of success obtained from a stunting defense cannot always be determined by the number of shots blocked or passes stolen. Changing the style and tempo of the game forces your opponents to play a type of game they have not practiced.

CONCENTRATING THE DEFENSE ON A SPECIFIC OFFENSIVE STRENGTH OF THE OPPOSING TEAM

Without the 20 or 30 points that some teams receive nightly from their "star," many teams are helpless. Here is another way to reap the profits from stunting defenses. Unfortunately for coaches, every team does not have that real tough defensive player who can "hook up" with the opposing team's offensive phenomenon and hold him 10 to 15 points below his average. Because of the present emphasis on the jump shot and the lightning speed of modern players, those "super scorers" are becoming harder and harder to defend. By using a combination defense, these seemingly unstoppable scorers can be halted.

Peck Hickman, the amiable and highly successful University of Louisville coach, once told the story of some advice that an old ladies' sewing circle gave him on how to stop Bradley's all-American scorer, Chet Walker. The presiding officer of the sewing circle phoned Coach Hickman's office to offer the following advice: "Play two men on Walker, then play the other four men man-for-man." Of course, basketball rules forbid such action, but the use of stunting defenses will often give you the same advantage of an additional defensive player.

COVERING UP A PARTICULAR DEFENSIVE WEAKNESS

Speed and quickness are two essentials of defensive excellence. All basketball players do not possess these skills. Nevertheless, by making the offense unsure of the type defense it is facing, the lack of speed and quickness can be covered. Also, there might be occasions when a key defender is injured slightly and cannot perform at full speed. A combination defense in this instance can prove most helpful, especially to the high school coach who is often faced with a lack of depth. Although such a situation might arise only once during the course of an entire season, the prospects of changing a seemingly sure defeat into victory are enough to warrant consideration of some sort of stunting defense by every coach.

Also, protecting a man with excessive fouls may be another reason for the use of a stunting defense.

Finally, you may be blessed with an outstanding big man who is too valuable under the boards to have your team employ a straight man-for-man defense. Thus you run the risk of having him pulled away from the boards. A stunting defense can alleviate this problem and keep him near the basket.

GIVING THE PLAYERS A PSYCHOLOGICAL BOOST BY DOING SOMETHING DIFFERENT

Basketball is a game of mental preparedness as well as physical preparation. The team whose morale is high will not be easily defeated. Coaches resort to various kinds of pre-game talks and other gimmicks in order to achieve the proper mental outlook for a forthcoming game. Adolph Rupp is a master at this sort of pre-game preparation. However, every coach is not endowed with this extraordinary ability. Also, some teams will not react to a verbal exhortation to victory. What then? Most coaches have a favorite method that they find particularly effective in getting their team up for a game. We have found special defensive preparation to be a most effective assurance of high morale for an upcoming game. Stunting defenses usually require an extra amount of concentration and effort on the part of the players. The psychological advantages of stunting defenses are enough to warrant consideration by the basketball coach. The coach whose team is an underdog can use alternating and combination defenses as a gimmick to instill confidence in a team facing sure defeat. Players tend to believe that this is the equalizer, that they will surprise the opponents if all assignments are carried out properly. An atmosphere of confidence will pervade the pre-game dressing quarters if each team member has worked diligently to learn his part in the execution of the defensive game plan.

The coach whose team possesses superior strength and has been labeled the "favorite" will find that he also can stunt his defenses at strategic points in the season, to give his players a boost for a game he feels is likely to be taken for granted by the team. Of course, one might ask why vary from the normal when success is apparent. The human factors that enter into the game of basketball make it difficult to predict future performance and morale. A team that has recently experienced a series of wins over strong opponents very conceivably could take a weaker opponent lightly and lose. Doing something different on defense will eliminate to some degree this take-it-for-granted attitude and provide the initiative and challenge to prevent such a reversal.

WEAKNESSES

Although the advantages of defensive stunting in basketball certainly outnumber the disadvantages, it is necessary to point out the disadvantages of such defenses so that you, as a coach, can recognize the pitfalls and traps in teaching these defenses. These disadvantages are:

1. Stunting defenses require more teaching time than conventional ones.
2. In most cases, a scout report is necessary.
3. There is the likelihood of creating a weakness that could be exploited if detected by the opposition.

Actually, the first two disadvantages may result from the overall organization of a particular basketball program over which the coach has no control. The third one results from specific weaknesses of each defense.

In order to implement successfully a defensive attack that will keep the offense guessing, two types of defenses must be taught. These defenses must, of necessity, be a man-for-man, (either switching or sliding) and any one of a number of zone defenses. We have found it best to teach only one zone and flex to match the offensive formation. The mechanics of the flexing zone will be explained in a later chapter. The man-for-man defense and zone defense must be taught as two separate entities, with the realization that the basic man-for-man principles should be mastered before any attempt is made at teaching the zone. Therefore, it is best to progress from individual defensive skills to team man-for-man skills, then to the zone.

Since this approach usually requires several weeks, the teams whose players are late in reporting to practice because of participation in autumn sports will find it unwise to stunt their defenses in the early part of the season. At best, midseason use would be the earliest conceivable date that the players could become conditioned so that they could react to the cues involved in stunting defenses and execute properly the basic principles of defensive maneuverability. Do not be too hasty in employing a stunting defense. The results could be disastrous.

A second weakness is that a scout report on the opposing team is almost necessary. It would not be practical to stunt defenses against a team about which you were uninformed. Only through careful study and analysis of the opponent's offensive attack can a stunting defense be organized and effectively implemented.

Scouting has become an important part of basketball. The coach who scouts gets more from his players. They know he is working, and in return work harder to satisfy the coach's demands.

The third weakness of stunting defenses is that occasionally a weakness is created that could be exploited if detected by the opposition. Of course, each defense can be effectively combatted

by the right offense. The sliding man-for-man can be exploited
by a screening offense. The switching man-for-man is weak
against the screen and roll. While a weakness is implicit in each
defense, the element of surprise will make a stunt effective for
a time.

Successful defensive teams are aware of their weaknesses.
They work to overcome any deficiencies which their particular
defensive system exposes by mastering the defensive fundamentals. These will be discussed in the next chapter.

2

Basic Defensive Skills

Good defensive play always reverts to sound man-for-man fundamentals. Regardless of the defense any team might use, no defense will function at its maximum effectiveness unless there has been a concentrated effort to master the smaller, perhaps less interesting phases of defense. Some of basketball's most successful coaches operate on the premise that it is not important what a team does, but how well that team performs a given task.

Championships have been won because teams have mastered and executed properly some of the most elementary and fundamental aspects of basketball. *Coach's Guide to Modern Basketball Defense* lists eight basic defensive fundamentals. These are: defensive break; stance and footwork; guarding the man with the ball; guarding the man without the ball; defending against offensive pivot play; defensive switching; sliding and blocking out for the rebound. Complete mastery of these skills provides a firm foundation for any defense a coach might wish to use. Repeated drills in these areas will provide for a hard-nosed team defense capable of adjusting to defend against any offense employed by opponents.

No coach wishes to become stagnant, refusing to acknowledge positive potentials in new trends. By combining the basic fundamentals of shooting with the new idea of jumping above the defense, the most effective and soundest shot in the game has been produced. The result has provided offensive fireworks beyond the fondest expectations. Likewise, new ideas on defense must first be preceded by a firm entrenchment of defensive fundamentals before coaches can use stunting defenses. With this realization in mind, let us look at some of the weaknesses that all successful defensive teams have overcome. The following basic defensive skills are fundamental considerations underlying the satisfactory implementation of any type of defense.

CHECKING THE FAST-BREAK

A team beaten down the floor repeatedly by the offense will never attain complete success from stunting defenses. Actually, defensive preparation begins on offense. A safety man or checker, as some call him, should be designated and given the primary responsibility of checking backcourt on rebound situations and at other times when there is a change in ball possession. Send one checker deep, about three or four steps from the head of the foul circle. Most likely, this will be a guard or the weakest rebounder. Designate another player as a shallow checker near the free-throw line. The shallow checker may pick up wide rebounds and loose balls coming his way. Also, he can still maintain position to beat the defense down the floor, aiding the deep checker in the event of an opponent's fast-break. Aggressive rebounding by the other three offensive men will help to prevent the fast-break situation.

Another method of making certain someone is always checking the offensive break is to assign cutters in the offensive pattern a secondary responsibility. Let a specific cutter become the defensive safety man when a shot is taken. For example, the third cutter in the Drake Shuffle would become the defensive safety man every time a shot is taken. This would be a different player most of the time, depending on where the continuity stops. In the first method, the deep safety man would be the same person every time.

Regardless of the method used, the point is clear. Someone must be backcourt to thwart the initial offensive approach of the opponents. Those players who are rebounders must sprint as fast as possible to the other end of the floor once it becomes apparent possession of the ball will not be retained on the rebound. The vital area from the free-throw line to the basket must be defended against the initial offensive thrust. Once the offensive break has been stopped, the defensive men move to their respective assignments.

Teams that make a smooth transition from offense to defense, then sprint quickly to the other end of the floor, will find their defenses becoming more effective. In order to stunt on defense, the defensive team must be one compact unit ready for the offensive approach.

Allot some time in each daily practice session to mastering the important skill of checking your opponent's fast-break. Divide your squad into teams of five. Have them run their offense from halfcourt without any defense, take a shot, and assume the correct rebound and safety positions. If the shot is missed, every effort should be made by the rebounders to put the ball back in the basket while the safety men or checkers maintain their

defensive positions. Once the shot is made, all five players
sprint to the opposite end of the floor. Their first obligation
is to protect the basket area against possible lay-up shots or
short jumps shots. After the initial offensive thrust has been
repelled, the players should move as quickly as possible to their
respective defensive assignments. While the first five returns
to the offensive end of the floor, have five more ready to move
on the floor and repeat the same procedure.

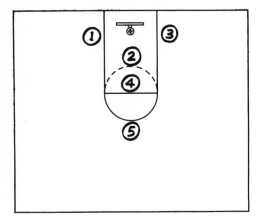

Diagram 1

In scrimmage emphasize, the importance of having someone
back to do the defensive checking. Check to see that each player
carries out his assignment. A good way to do this is to ask
players not involved in the scrimmage to keep a record of the
times when no one checked, and who failed to do so.

When the first method is used, the shallow checker on the
free-throw line can free-lance if he sees that he has a better
chance of getting the rebound than those nearer the basket.
However, he must realize his first responsibility is to give

strength to the deep checker. He does this by discouraging the quick outlet pass, by picking off wide rebounds and by getting down the floor fast.

Some teams choose to begin their fast-break by tipping the ball to a designated player near the free-throw line. Placing a shallow checker in this area will discourage such tactics.

Diagram 1 shows the ideal position when the shallow checker and deep safety man are used. The rebounders, O-1, O-2, O-3, form a triangle or a cup near the basket. O-4 is the shallow checker and O-5 the deep safety man. The number of offensive rebounders should be indicated before game time. Against teams who always bring the ball down the floor slowly, there may be no need to have both a shallow and deep checker. Against some teams, you may be able to send all five players to the offensive boards. Rest assured, however, that such a situation will rarely exist.

GUARD DEFENSE

The type of guard defense you employ should be the next consideration after the opponent's fast-break attempt has been stymied. Stunting defenses depend on the cohesiveness of all five defensive players. There must be a general understanding as to where to expect the strongest threat, so that compensation can be made. Guard defense is important, because deep penetration will wreck a defense before it can start to function properly. Force teams to initiate their offense farther out than they normally do.

Some teams attempt to turn the ball to the sidelines by over-playing the guards one-half man to the inside of the court. This method should produce a better angle to play cutters moving toward the ball. Of course, this could result in the dribbler eluding his defensive man and driving the baseline for an easy field goal. Once the dribbler gets a step on his defensive man down the sideline, there is little chance of recovery.

Diagram 2 shows X-1 overplaying O-1, the dribbler, to the inside. Notice the poor passing angle O-1 has to his other four teammates.

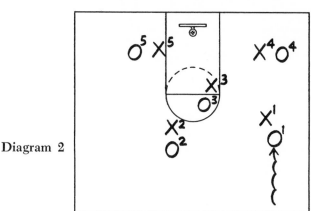

Diagram 2

Other teams try to turn the ball to the middle of the court by slightly overplaying the ball-handler's outside leg. By driving the dribbler to the middle of the floor, the defensive players are in a position to help each other, since the middle is where the defense is strongest and more compact. Also, turning the ball to the middle provides an excellent opportunity to double-team the ball without severely weakening the defense. We favor this type of backcourt defensive play.

In Diagram 3, notice the position of X-2 and X-5. They are in a position to help stop O-1, should X-1's overplay allow the dribbler sufficient room to drive toward the basket. Also, X-4 is in position to help.

There is still a third line of thinking concerning guard defense. Some coaches prefer to overplay the dribbler's strong hand and force him to use his weak hand. A right-hander would be forced to dribble with his left hand, and a left-hander would be forced to use his right hand. No consideration is given to the position of the dribbler on the court.

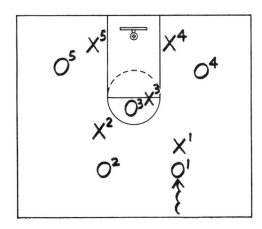

Diagram 3

In a recent poll conducted by *Scholastic Coach,* 15 leading college coaches in the U. S. were asked the question: "How do you influence a man in the backcourt? Do you try to force him to the outside or down the middle?" Six of these coaches preferred to force the offensive player to the outside. Four coaches said they felt it best to show the offense a slight advantage to the middle. Three coached their teams to guard the backcourt man in both manners, depending on strengths and weaknesses as revealed by their scouting reports. The other two coaches chose a third alternative—overplaying the strong hand of the dribbler.

As you can see, opinions on this matter vary. Regardless of the method you choose, choose one, stick with it, and work hard to perfect it. The effectiveness with which the dribbler is guided and stopped, plays an important role in the successful use of any stunting defense.

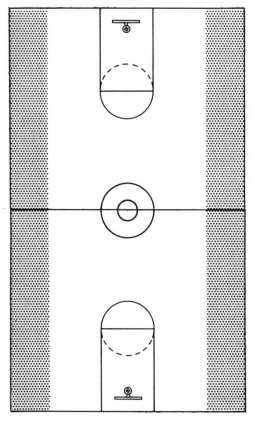

Diagram 4

There is generally a consensus of opinion among most coaches as to the most effective method of playing the dribbler in the backcourt when employing a pressure defense. Most have found it advantageous to overplay the dribbler's inside leg and force him toward the sideline, creating a double-team situation. Interceptions are easier, and the sideline area is an excellent place to execute the double-team. The shaded area in Diagram 4 represents the best double-team area.

GUARDING THE BASELINE

A great many defensive weaknesses develop in the area from the "free-throw line extended" to the baseline. Mistakes in this

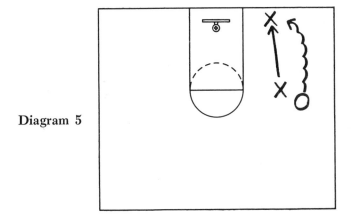

Diagram 5

critical area will make shambles of a defense. Defending the dribbler as he attempts to drive the baseline and guarding cutters in this area frequently create defensive problems.

We have discovered only one effective means of guarding the dribbler on an attempted drive down the baseline. First of all, overplay the baseline leg of any player you think might be a baseline threat. We hope to discourage moves toward the baseline. If a player does drive the baseline and it is apparent the defense has erred, the defensive player must attempt a cut-off by assuming a position facing the approaching driver at a point approximately one-half the distance between the basket and where the drive originated. Correct position on the part of defensive player, when contact occurs, will result in an offensive charging foul. These charging fouls can add a number of valuable ball possessions throughout the course of the season.

Diagram 5 shows the correct defensive position when guarding a man in the frontcourt who is attempting to score by driving the baseline.

PLAYING MEN WITHOUT THE BALL

We have spent hours preparing for the use of a stunting defense only to see the defense fold completely. Even though the dribbler was played expertly in the backcourt and the baseline drives were stopped, loose defensive play on the players who were not in possession of the ball destroyed the effectiveness of the defense. The other four men must do a good job of playing the men without the ball.

High school playing time is 32 minutes. If each team kept possession of the ball approximately half the game, then no one player could have the ball in his possession more than an average of 3.2 minutes per game. This means that each defensive man should be prepared to spend 8 to 12 minutes per high school game guarding a man who does not have possession of the basketball. In a college game, each player would average 4 minutes of ball possession. Each defensive man would find himself playing 16 minutes of defensive basketball guarding a man who does not have possession of the ball.

The importance of guarding the man without the ball cannot be overemphasized. Players tend to relax when they face a situation that does not involve the ball. A quick sag to the basket with an alert, aggressive movement will reduce your opponent's scoring opportunities. In Diagram 6, the weak-side sag position is indicated. Notice how much easier X-1 could avoid an off-ball screen.

While the defensive men who are not guarding the ball sag to the basket, pressure on the ball is a must. Play him tight if he has dribbled, and loose if he has not.

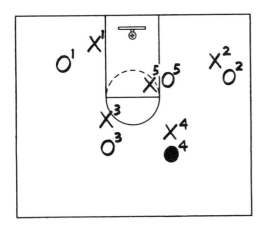

Diagram 6

Playing cutters properly will eliminate many of your defensive problems. Overplay all cutters into the three-second area about one-half step in the direction of the ball. Do not allow a cutter to receive a pass at the spot he would like to. Sometimes the cutter can be forced wider by body checking. Stepping in front of players and drawing the offensive charging foul has provoked a more aggressive brand of defensive play in our area.

Many basketball players are phenomenal when they have the ball in their possession, but they find themselves lost when they do not have the ball. Few players are skilled in the art of getting open when they are without the ball. Stunting defenses will yield fewer points if the cutters and other men without the ball are overplayed so they find it difficult to receive a pass.

DEFENSING THE TALL PIVOT MAN

Defensing teams with a tall pivot man is a problem every coach must cope with. Whenever possible, it is best to match a tall pivot man with a tall defensive man, but since a "jolly giant" does not always grace every coach's squad, stunting defenses will provide an effective means of stopping the big man's scoring maneuvers.

The best defense against the good pivot man is never to allow him to receive a pass in the pivot-post area. Play the pivot man on the side nearest the ball. Occasionally, play directly in front of the post man, but this gives the offense the inside position on the rebound and also makes the defense vulnerable to the lob pass. For this reason, determine the greatest strength of the opposing pivot man—will he hurt you more with his shooting and driving than with his offensive rebounding and tipping? If a pivot man is a definite threat on the offensive boards, you should hesitate to relinquish the inside rebounding position by playing in front of him. On the other hand, if a pivot man is a dangerous scoring threat from the floor, play him tight on the side nearest the ball, trying to keep the ball away from him. A good sag by the weak-side defensive men will help to eliminate some of the problems involved in defending the big men. Any one-on-one situation near the basket is dangerous. Try to avoid such situations.

SELL THE PLAYERS

The last basic defensive maneuver to be considered is perhaps more of a mental exercise than a physical one. Sell your players on the over-all value of defense, then sell them on the importance of the stunting defense you are preparing. Be certain everyone on the team, subs included, knows and understands every move. Do not take the floor when ill-prepared. Spend at least one-third of your practice rehearsing defensive fundamentals and practicing the different types of defenses you plan to use.

A solid grounding in the fundamental phases of defense will allow you to do more things with your defense. It will allow you to throw the unusual at your opponents and give you the satisfaction of having done your best to prepare your team for victory.

3

Flexing Zone Defense

Since basketball fundamentals and tactical situations require more and more practice time, coaches are finding it difficult to cover all phases of the game as thoroughly as they would like. In days past, teams incorporating a zone defense usually developed at least two such defenses, most often the 2-1-2 and the 1-3-1. A third, usually a 1-2-2, was often used for insurance—total preparation for any type offense.

Now, coaches find there is not enough time in the daily practice schedule to develop a zone defense to match every offense. As a result, some teams depend entirely on their man-for-man defense to carry them through the season. The strict man-for-man proves to be a great disadvantage. Opposing teams can concentrate entirely on their screening offense, which likely will make them more effective than if they were forced to prepare for more than one defense. Also, there are some teams that do not attack zone defenses well. It seems a shame to place all of your defensive eggs in one basket by completely ignoring the zone.

ADVANTAGES OF THE FLEXING ZONE

The flexing zone defense will give you a multiple defense that can be used against a number of attacks. It offers the advantages of several different defenses in one and will curtail the amount of time spent developing defenses.

The team that continually changes its pattern in an attempt to overload or exploit a certain zone's weaknesses won't be able to do this against the flexing zone. Against a zone with an odd front, most teams attack offensively with an even number front. They use an odd man front against a zone with an even number defensive front. The flexing zone will eliminate the problem of calling time out to change defenses. After recognizing the offense, the defensive players adjust, matching the offense man-for-man and defending with zone and man-for-man principles.

DEVELOPING A FLEXING ZONE DEFENSE

When developing such a defense, any of the standard zone formations may be used as the basic defense. We have found

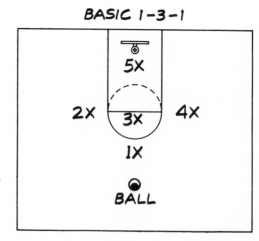

BASIC 1-3-1

Diagram 7

SLIDES TO THE RIGHT

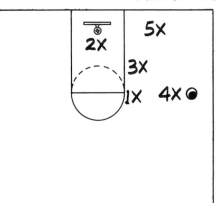 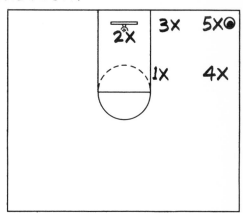

Diagram 8   Diagram 9

the 1-3-1 to be most effective because of the simplicity of its slides. The 1-3-1 zone and its basic slides are shown in Diagrams 7-11.

SLIDES TO THE LEFT

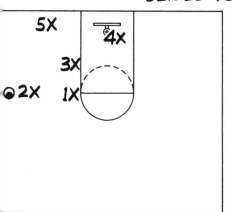 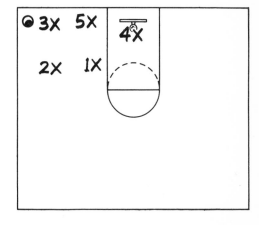

Diagram 10   Diagram 11

SLIDES TO THE LEFT

The slides are the same to both sides of the floor, except for the corner positions. When the ball goes to the left corner,

OVERLOAD TO LEFT

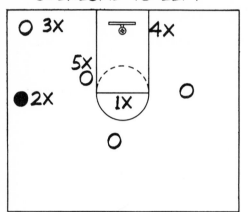

Diagram 12

X3 plays the ball (Diagram 11) and X5 assumes the second position in the line of three men between the ball and the

OVERLOAD TO RIGHT

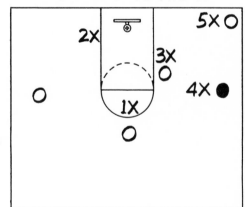

Diagram 13

basket. Because of the distance involved in moving from one corner to the other when one man is assigned both corners to cover, X5 is assigned the right corner (Diagram 9). X3 takes the number two position. This will allow either man to cheat slightly toward his corner when the offense overloads in that direction.

In the event a 1-3-1 offensive formation is used, no flex is necessary to match the offense. Coverage of the 1-3-1 formation is shown in Diagrams 12 and 13.

Flexing from the 1-3-1 against the 2-1-2 or the 1-2-2

Most teams will attack a 1-3-1 zone with either a 2-1-2 or a 1-2-2 offensive formation. The 1-3-1 zone can be flexed to match

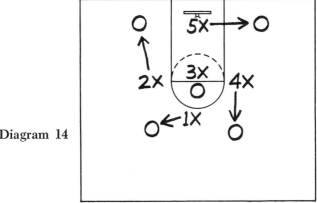

Diagram 14

these offensive threats. The flex may become automatic when a two-man front is seen, or it can be made more mechanically through the use of a signal given by a defensive quarterback.

You might choose to make the adjustment at a time out. Best results are obtained when the flex is automatic. The defense should also be aware of any change in the offensive position on the baseline and free-throw line. These are the points at which a 1-2-2 offense will differ from a 1-3-1 offense.

To cope with the threat of the 2-1-2 offensive formation, have the defensive players match the offensive players nearest their original zone area. (See Diagram 14.)

With each man flexing to cover the offensive threats in different areas, the defense now resembles a 2-1-2 zone. When the ball is in the right corner, X5 takes the corner, X3 assumes the

BALL IN RIGHT CORNER

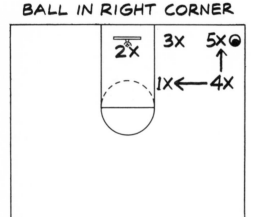

Diagram 15

second position, and X2 takes the goal, thus keeping three men in line between the ball and the basket. (See Diagram 15.) X1 pinches toward the middle to protect this vital area with X3. X4 has three alternatives. He may double-team the ball in the corner, overplay the receiver in the area of the free-throw line extended, or pinch to the middle and help out with a dangerous pivot man. X2 has the same alternatives at his discretion when the ball is in the left corner. In our pre-game preparation, we determine exactly how the wingmen (X2 and X4) will slide.

BALL IN LEFT CORNER

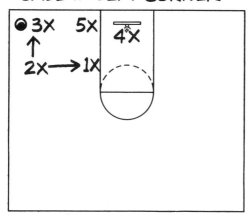

Diagram 16

If the ball were in the left corner, X3 would play the ball, X5 would take the second position, and X4 the third or rebounding position under the basket. X1 would slide to the middle and help out as he did on the other side of the floor. X2 would either doube-team, sag to the middle, or overplay the receiver.

When the offensive team chooses to employ a 1-2-2 formation, the middle man (X3) simply drops back to a position on the baseline opposite X5, who has flexed slightly to a position on the right side of the key. The other defensive players keep their same positions. The offensive positions are matched with a minimum shifting of the defense. (See Diagram 17.) The two-on-one situation, which initially prevailed under the basket, has been eliminated. As the ball moves around the perimeter of the defense, the players take the same slides they took in the basic 1-3-1 zone.

We feel that if we can successfully defend against the 1-3-1, the 2-1-2, and the 1-2-2 offensive formations, we are prepared to cope with almost any situation that will arise. By making slight adjustments in pre-game preparations, the flexing zone can easily be adapted to any type of offense, including unorthodox formations. Occasionally, we work against some of these unorthodox formations in case there should ever be a need to defense one.

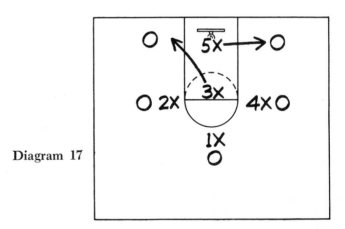

Diagram 17

At this point, it may be well to add that we never use the flexing zone unless we feel that we can stay fairly close to the basic slides of our 1-3-1 zone. We do not want to belabor the players with a number of complicated "match-ups." Instead, we want them to concentrate on quick, aggressive movement, holding foremost in their mind the thought that everything in their power will be done to stifle the opposing team's scoring threat. The slides of the flexing zone should be smooth and fluid.

The 2-3 and the 2-2-1 Give the Flexing 1-3-1 Trouble

Two of the formations we have found most difficult to adjust to without breeching the rules of the basic 1-3-1 are a 2-3 and a 2-2-1. (See Diagrams 18 and 19.)

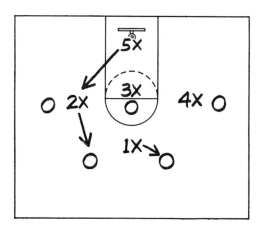

Diagram 18

These match-ups must be governed by a different set of rules. In Diagram 18, X5 has been pulled away from the basket-baseline area that he customarily has covered. The basket area is left open, eliminating one of the advantages of a zone—protection of the high percentage shooting area. In Diagram 19,

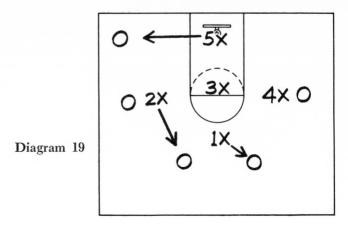

Diagram 19

X5 is pulled into the corner normally guarded by X3. X3 is forced to cover X2's area.

IMPORTANCE OF THE FLEXING ZONE

The flexing zone has become the heart of basketball's stunting defenses. Someday it will probably evolve into a type of rule defense. Since the flexing zone requires each defensive player to play the man in his area man-for-man, movement of players on offense has necessitated the implementation of a few basic rules to cover all situations. The flexing zone operates more effectively against an offense in which the players remain relatively static. If an offensive player dribbles, the defensive man who has matched up with him stays with the offensive player until he dribbles into another defensive zone. When he has been picked up by another defensive player, he then assumes the correct floor position in relation to the ball. If an offensive player cuts to the basket or the ball, the defensive man overplays the cutter as far as the three-second area, then assumes his correct floor position.

SIX DEFENSIVE PRINCIPLES OF THE FLEXING ZONE

There are several other factors contributing to the success of the flexing zone. These six principles will help to establish a sound defense:

1. Beat the offense down the floor.
2. Keep the hands and arms extended at all times. This will discourage shots and passes, especially long passes that will shatter a zone.
3. Recognize the offense and flex to match it before the ball penetrates. Guard the man in your area man-for-man.
4. Do not allow the ball to be passed into the middle. Overplay offensive players stationed on or near the free-throw line so they cannot receive the ball.
5. Do not give teams a good outside shot. Always put a hand in the shooter's face.
6. After a shot is taken, block out for the rebound.

4

Alternating Defenses

Basketball has moved from the man-for-man defense to zone defenses, to sloughing man-for-man defenses, to zone combination defenses, and to alternating defenses. Until Hank Luisetti popularized the one-hand push shot and someone decided to jump before shooting the one-hander, little was done to confuse the offensive efforts of the opposition. Alternating defenses are among the latest innovations in the modern swing to defense. A team will change from one defense to another on successive trips to the defensive end of the floor. The strategy is to make the offense vary its attack so that no definite pattern can be established. Offensive execution, as a result, will not be as sharp.

UPSET OFFENSIVE RHYTHM

Alternating defenses tend to throw the offense off its regular rhythm. They are particularly effective against teams that depend on pattern moves to free them for a shot. Doubt and confusion as to the type of defense they are facing will increase the number of times the offense will lose the ball without taking a good shot.

The alternations may consist of a number of defenses. An alternation involving the various zone formations can prove discouraging to a team whose zone attack is presenting a problem. If the 2-1-2 is your basic zone defense, have your team employ that defense several times at the beginning of the game. About the time the offensive team starts to attack the zone well, a different zone can be thrown at them on a prearranged signal. The second zone may be selected from any number of zone defenses, depending on the one that will best stop the offense. After one or two plays, the initial zone can be reinstated. In most cases, it is best to alternate only two defenses, because players will become confused if more than two are used.

SWITCHING FROM MAN-TO-MAN TO ZONE

One of the most effective alternations is the change from a man-for-man defense to a zone. In our case, we prefer the switching man-for-man and the flexing zone. Either one may be used as the starting defense. The objective is to confuse the offense and catch them attacking the zone with a man-for-man offense or attacking the man-for-man defense with a zone offense. Any type of man-for-man and zone defense will suffice; however, it is advisable to use a zone defense matching the opposing team's offensive alignment.

Suppose the opposition depends to a large extent on the Drake Shuffle. (See Diagram 20.) Since its alignment is closer

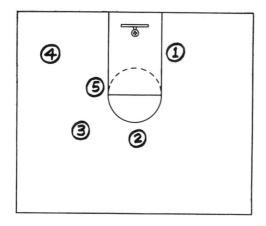

Diagram 20

to a 2-1-2 formation than anything else, a rotation between a 2-1-2 zone and a man-for-man defense could be used. By flexing slightly, the zone can cover all men. Diagram 21 shows the coverage on the man-for-man rotation.

The various types of man-for-man defense afford several stunts with which to vary your defensive play. Use of the switching and sliding principles on an alternating basis is an effective way of confusing the offense, especially free-lance

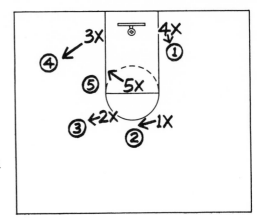

Diagram 21

teams. Using cues to be described later in this chapter, the defense switches in all situations where two offensive players cross. When a signal is given, the defense slides on all crosses. Only a well-disciplined defensive team can react to this type of alternation because it requires an absolute understanding of the defenses involved.

DEFENSIVE GUARD PLAY

Defensive guard play is in many cases the key to the over-all success of team defensive play. Cincinnati's Tony Yates, called by Coach Ed Jucker "the greatest defensive player in collegiate basketball," is proof enough of what defensive guard play can do for a team. He and his running mate at the other guard position have badgered and harassed more than one team into submission with their fierce guard play.

If the guards will vary their attack, the offense will not be apt to get set. Driving the offensive guards to the middle for a while, then showing them the outside, helps to keep pressure on them. It continually forces the offense to change and adjust to cope with the style of play as set up by the defense.

Guards Should Work Together

The two guards can work together in alternating their defensive play. Their work is as important to a basketball team as the shortstop-second baseman combination is to a baseball team. The keystone combination needs to be aware of every move the other half of the combo makes. Most baseball teams devise a simple set of signals that allows the shortstop and second baseman to know who will cover the base in every situation. Likewise, in basketball, the defensive guards need to communicate and work together as they try to thwart the initial drive of the offense.

Defensive guard play is so important because teams tend to practice without any sort of harassment. In an effort to work on timing, cuts, and screens, many teams fail to practice against one of the most important elements of the game—initiation of their offense. For this reason, you can provide some frustrating moments by alternating pressure on the offensive guards. Have your guards pick up the offensive guards at centerline for a few plays, then fall back and pick up a few steps out from the head of the circle. Occasionally, pick up the guards down under their defensive basket. This type of pressure and harassment throughout the game will break their rhythm and result in more poor percentage shots plus a higher number of possession turn-overs.

Ball-Stealing Not Paramount

While it is a challenge to try to take the ball away when applying pressure, you must remember that this is not the sole objective. In fact, we like to encourage our players to refrain from slapping and stealing the ball. Mistakes will come. Most players dislike defensive pressure. We want to wait and allow the offense to make the mistake. Foolish fouls destroy the effectiveness of halfcourt pressure. Slashing and slapping for the ball may yield a few quick points at the outset of the game, but in the late stages, when your best defensive player is needed, you may find him seated beside you on the bench, disqualified by personal fouls.

WAYS TO MAKE THE CHANGE

These are some of the changes that may be used in the alternation of defenses. Your own ingenuity may produce more. However, the type of defense used is not always as important as the change itself. Every defensive player must be aware that a change in defensive assignments is being made. If some hang to their man-for-man responsibilities while other players are zoning, the effectiveness of alternating defenses will be lost.

A team well-versed in defensive fundamentals, and knowing when to change defenses, will present a stout barrier to any offensive team. With this in mind, let us look at different methods that can be used to cue a defensive alternation.

Time Out

The most obvious way to alternate defenses is through the use of the time out. During the time out, instruct your players to use a specific defense until the next time out is called. Later in the game, use a second time out to change to another defense. Try to make the change just as the opposing team indicates it has solved your defense and begins to make adjustments in its attack. Such a system limits the number of alternations that can be made, since it is not practical to reserve time outs solely for the purpose of changing the defense. Also, it is important to save several time outs for the latter stages of the game. To be effective over the entire course of the game, alternating defenses need to be changed more often than the use of this method will allow.

Signals from the Bench

A more practical way to alternate defenses is to give the signals directly from the bench. These cues may be given by voice and position of the hand and other parts of the body. Musical instruments can also serve as a gimmick to cue a defensive change. Bench signals are particularly effective when benches are located at the end of the playing court. When the bench is on the opposite end of the defensive court, hand signals or some other visual signal is best. During the half, when your defense forms near the bench, the signal can be given as the players retreat to their defensive position, or a verbal signal can be given after the defense gets downcourt and backs are turned to the bench. When the players' bench is located along the sidelines, any type of signal may be used depending on the playing environment.

Crowded, noisy conditions will sometimes make it impossible for you to use verbal signals. Though the coach is generally close enough to the playing area to be heard by his players, the rumble and roar of the crowd will often muffle his voice. When conditions do allow you to use verbal cues, call the defense by its name or use a number, letter, or some other symbol. For example, the number "one" might be the cue for a 1-3-1 zone, and the number "two" could indicate a change to a 2-1-2 zone. A man-for-man and zone alternation could be cued by having any number over 20 signal a zone defense. Any number under 20 would signal the man-for-man defense.

Rehearse these cues in practice under actual game conditions, with plenty of noise in the gym. The players might react perfectly in the quietness and solitude of the practice environment, but fail to do so under actual game conditions because they could not distinguish the cue. If there is any doubt as to whether or not the players will be able to hear your voice, abandon the idea and look for another cue.

Hand signals are a good way to solve problems caused by noisy gyms. One finger extended could call for a 1-3-1 zone, two fingers a 2-1-2 zone. A clenched fist might be the signal for a man-for-man. Since these cues are so simple, the offense is apt to catch them and adjust to the type of defense being used against them. If the coach is in a good position to be seen by his players, other signals will be more practical. Crossing the legs for a man-for-man defense, uncrossing them for a zone defense is so closely related to natural movements of the body that it would be difficult for the offense to catch the cue.

Since a number of coaches like to fidget with a towel while the game is in progress, this anxiety-absorbent makes a good signal for alternating defenses. A towel over your shoulder or across your knees is one series of signals that can be used when alternating between a man-for-man and zone defense. Prerequisites for this method are a bright-colored towel, a quick glance by the players as they set up their defense, and a disciplined rehearsal in practice.

Musical Instruments

One of the most successful system of cues for alternating defenses is the use of a musical instrument. At Oglethorpe, we were blessed with one of the loudest and most spirited pep bands to be found anywhere. The trumpet player took great pride in releasing loud blasts on his horn at intervals throughout the game. The shattering noises from his horn could be heard no matter how enthusiastic the crowd was. One night, against a state rival, our strategy was to alternate from a man-for-man defense to a 2-1-2 zone. The cue was to be a blast from the horn. So effectively did the alternating defenses stymie the rival's offensive patterns, we were able to defeat them for the first time in Oglethorpe's history. However, the story of the horn blasts did not end with that victory. The newspapers picked up the story and passed it along to the rest of our opponents. Realizing that opposing teams might expect us to use the same trick on them, we always had the trumpet player available for duty. Occasionally, the same signal was used to alternate defenses but mostly the bugle was only a threat. The trumpet player's presence at the game was enough to convince people that something different in the way of defensive play was to be unfolded that night.

In some instances, the trumpet player gave a loud blast with his horn, but before the game we had determined such sounds would mean nothing. The opposing team, having read about the horn scheme in the newspaper, immediately called time on several occasions to make offensive adjustments for an alternating defense we never used.

The Score

Another effective method of alternating defenses is to let the score cue the change. As long as the score remains on even digits, use one defense. When the score is an odd number, employ a different defense. Location of the scoreboard is an important consideration, since the players will not always have time to turn and look for the score as the offense to defense change-over is made.

A strong start at the beginning of a game often proves to be the difference. How many games have you seen when one team jumps to a quick lead, but never builds or adds to that lead as the game progresses? The teams merely exchange baskets throughout the game. For some reason, a number of basketball games follow that trend. The opening minutes can be decisive. Because of this, an unexpected defense in the first few minutes of play might mean some compromising adjustments by your opponents. The objective is to upset their normal game long enough to build up a lead.

You might open with an aggressive zone, in the hope of taking advantage of some early ball-handling mistakes. When the opposing team scores six points, have your team fall back into a predetermined defense. Challenge your team to see how long they can defend without allowing the opposition to score a fixed number of points.

An early lead will instill confidence and boost your team's morale considerably. Most people are front runners by nature. They do not like to come from behind.

Field Goals and Free Throws

Field goals and free throws can be used to cue defensive alternations. Either the opposition's free throws and field goals can be used to make changes or you can use your own. Let us use our own field goals and free throws in setting up a hypothetical case. Start the game in a man-for-man defense. Remain in that defense until your team scores a field goal. When the field goal is scored, have the players automatically change to another defense. Stay in that defense until another field goal is scored. The same alternation can be made with the free throw serving as the cue. Remember, on all missed shots, there is no change. The alternation occurs only after a shot has been made. In situations where there are two free throws, let the last one determine the change. If it is missed, stay in the same defense.

Defensive Quarterback

In some situations, a defensive quarterback can serve as the cue for defensive changes. The player who is given this responsibility can call for alternations with oral signals, hand signals,

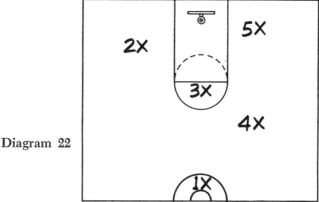

Diagram 22

or by indicating a change according to the position on the floor that he assumes while waiting for the offense to come down the

floor. The oral and hand signals of the defensive quarterback
should resemble closely those used by the coach from the bench.

If you wanted to rotate three defenses during a game by using
a defensive player's position on the floor as a cue, divide the
court into three areas. Let each area of the court have a relationship to a specific defense. For example, when the defensive
quarterback (X1) lines up in the center-jump circle (see Diagram 22), a halfcourt pressing man-for-man defense would be
used. When he stations himself between the center circle and
the top of the free-throw circle (see Diagram 23), a normal
man-for-man would be used. And when he positions himself

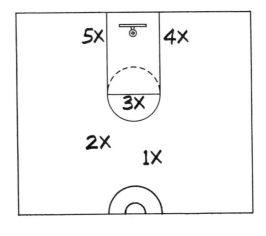

Diagram 23

inside the free-throw circle (see Diagram 24), a zone defense
would be used.

The defensive quarterback preferably should be a guard.
The guards are usually in a position where they can be seen

better by the other players. The pivot man is usually the second-best person to direct the defense, especially if hand signals or verbal signals are to be used. It would be difficult for him to change floor position to signal a change.

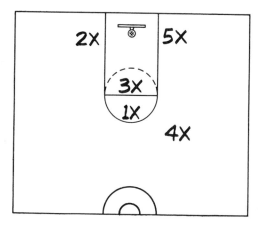

Diagram 24

Alternating defenses through a defensive quarterback is an excellent way to use a boy who lacks a little in offensive ability. Placing the responsibility on him to change defenses increases his feeling of value to the team and gives him a greater feeling of contributing to the over all team effort.

Some teams that rely heavily on offensive patterns like to use hand and verbal signals to call their plays. As they come to the offensive end of the floor, one of the players, most likely a guard, will raise his hand or call a number to indicate the series of patterns to be run. A team capable of initiating its pattern methods other than by hand or verbal signals can confuse the opposition by using these same cues to call its defenses while it actually is on offense. Have one of your offensive guards give the signal just after he crosses the centerline. The defense will think your signals are setting offensive patterns. When you score or lose possession of the ball, your defense will set up according to the signal given on offense. The defense remains the same until another signal is given.

The Offensive Pattern of the Opponent

Many teams predicate their attack upon a pass to the forwards. They need to make this first pass in order to get their offense rolling. In the event you are able to detect an initiation pattern of this nature, you might want to alternate defenses by zoning when the initiation pass goes to the left side and playing a man-for-man when the pass goes to the right side. In a sense, the offense is determining the alternations for you.

When a defense of this type is used, meet the initial offensive approach with a man-for-man defense. Thus every man will be covered as your opponents scramble for position. Once the initial pass cues the defensive change, the defense remains in that defense until the next time down the floor. Make sure every player understands he is to play the same defense, even though the offense resets after an unsuccessful field goal attempt. On passes to the post man, have everyone stay with his man. Do not change defenses on this pass.

Game Situations

One alternation we have found handy is determined by game situations, rather than any particular cue. On many occasions, a game will go into the last minute of play and we will be trailing by one point or more. As long as we trail, the half-court pressing zone is our defense. As soon as we get ahead, we change back to our normal man-for-man defense. When we get behind, we feel it best to gamble to get ahead. Since the halfcourt pressing zone produces good double-team situations and places men in position to intercept, we feel safer in a close game to use it rather than the full-court press.

SUMMARY

Some of the ideas on alternating defenses are complex; many of them are simple. The fact that your opponents will know you are capable of throwing several defenses at them during a game is enough to warrant serious consideration of their uses.

5

Combination Defenses

A generally accepted practice among members of the coaching profession is to reserve the unusual for teams of superior strength. All of us look for the equalizer. Although strength can never be overcome by weakness, careful planning and imaginative strategy make it possible to defeat stronger opponents. Combination defenses are a part of the overall season planning, but they do not necessarily need to be stored away for stronger teams. They can be as instrumental in defeating a team of equal or less ability as they can in upsetting the favorite.

STIMULATES INTEREST IN DEFENSE

We have found that using combination defenses and other stunting defenses stimulates interest in defense. They help to build team pride. The players enjoy arranging a pre-game defensive plan and following through with it. They work harder to perfect the defensive variation to be used.

Combination defenses can be used to stop the high-scoring "superstar" or to clog up offensive pattern work. The box-and-one, triangle-and-two, and the diamond-and-one are familiar to every coach and basketball player. It is hard to be exposed to the game for any length of time without coming into contact with one of these defenses. They are designed to force the offense into a mode of play they are unaccustomed to. Their objective is to make the offense operate against a defense for which they have not practiced.

Some coaches question the use of these defenses. They doubt if these combination zone and man-for-man defenses are important enough to spend the amount of time required to perfect them. Actually, these defenses can be installed in a comparatively short time if they are compatible with your basic defenses. Stay as close to the fundamentals principles as possible.

The 1-3-1 zone principles are employed in the following combination defenses regardless of how many defensive players are zoning. The same rules concerning switching, sliding and other man-for-man fundamentals are employed by the players who are given man-for-man assignments. Instead of teaching a completely new defense, your job is simplified to the task of coordinating parts of two separate defenses.

ZONE-AND-ONE VARIATIONS

Joe Dean in his travels for Converse Rubber Company calls the real fine defensive player a "good glove man." The connotations of the term are borrowed from baseball lingo where the flashy fielders are glamorized as "good glove men." However, when talking about defense and its importance to the game, Joe's description of the outstanding defensive player seems to carry broader implications. The tough defensive player covers the offensive situation like a glove covers the hand.

When it comes to stopping an opposing team's high scorer, the ideal way is to assign a "good glove man" that task, then sit back and watch the battle. Nowhere in athletics is there a challenge surpassing this one. One on one, man against man, who is the best? Every coach dreams about having that one reliable defensive player capable of turning in such a performance. Unfortunately, we seldom find a defender of this quality. Even when one is discovered, he operates under the disadvantage of never knowing when his man will dribble, shoot, or pass. Also, you may not be able to match the top scorer with size and speed. Regardless of how good a little man is, he will find it almost impossible to whip a good big man. The zone-and-one can be the equalizer in some instances. It helps to limit the phenom's scoring opportunities.

Variation of the Flexing 1-3-1

The zone-and-one is nothing more than a variation of the flexing 1-3-1 zone. The zone's original formation can be that of a diamond or box. (See Diagrams 25 and 26.) The middle man (X3) becomes the player who is assigned the responsibility of guarding the opposing team's top scoring threat. All the other

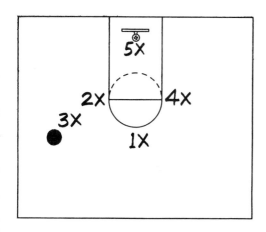

Diagram 25

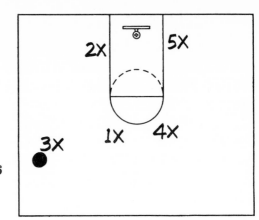

Diagram 26

defensive players have the same responsibility they normally would have in the 1-3-1 zone, even to the point of flexing to match different offensive formations. By flexing, the zone-and-one can easily become a box-and-one instead of a diamond-and-one.

Needs Good Defensive Player in the Middle

Because this adjustment is a part of the over-all strategy, try to put a good defensive player in the middle position when developing your zone defense. Personnel differences may necessi-

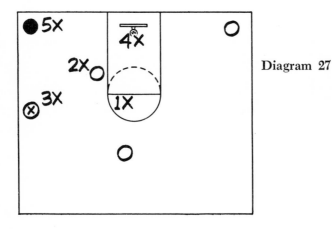

Diagram 27

tate the assignment of someone other than the middle man to guard the "hotshot." Make as few changes as possible by bringing the middle man out to replace the defensive zone man who has been given the man-for-man assignment.

The only other change in defensive responsibility is to give the goalie (X5) both corners to cover. Here is the way to cover when the ball is in the corner. (See Diagrams 27 and 28.) Use

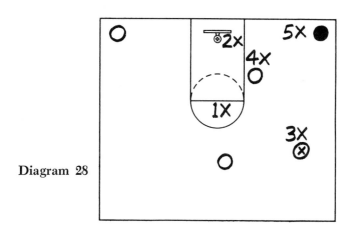

Diagram 28

the same slides if the defense is a box-and-one. (See Diagrams 29 and 30.)

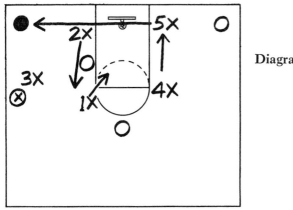

Diagram 29

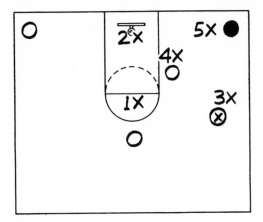

Diagram 30

When the ball is at the wing position coverage from both formations is the same. (See Diagrams 31 and 32.)

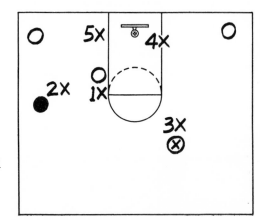

Diagram 31

The four men who are zoning are concerned primarily with the critical scoring area. They should not permit an unmolested shot from the outside, however. Quick movement will force the shooters to hurry their shots. Keeping the arms extended helps to close the gap created when the middle man vacates that position to assume his man-for-man assignment.

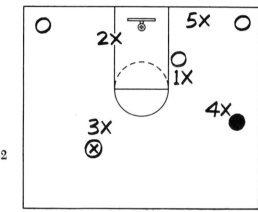

Diagram 32

The middle man's major objective is to keep his man from receiving the ball. Of course, it will be impossible to keep it away from him for the complete game. But the fewer times he is allowed to receive the ball, the fewer scoring opportunities he will have.

Defensing the Good Pivot Man

So far nothing has been said about stopping the good inside man. Remarks have been limited to defensing perimeter players. By this we mean offensive players who play away from the basket. Defending the tough pivot man has become one of the hardest jobs on the basketball court. The big men in the game today are so mobile and strong they can hardly be stopped.

We have found the 1-3-1 zone to be an effective defense against the big man. This is one reason for making it our basic zone defense. If possible we like to defend against the big man by using the normal 1-3-1 without stunts or other adjustments. Sometimes there is just not enough height on our defensive team, so we make one simple adjustment on the 1-3-1 that provides adequate defense against most pivot attacks.

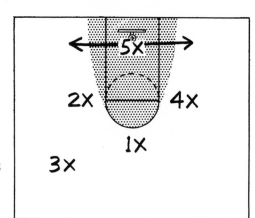

Diagram 33

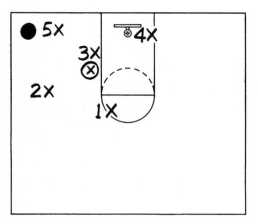

Diagram 34

The middle man on the 1-3-1 zone is assigned the responsibility of guarding the pivot man anywhere he goes within a 15 foot radius of the goal. The goalie (X5) is responsible for both corners. These two adjustments yield a diamond zone, with one defender harrassing the pivot man in the heart of the diamond. When the ball is in the corner, there will be no one to fill the number two defensive position on the baseline. (See Diagram 34.)

The shaded area in Diagram 33 is the general area in which the really good pivot man should be played on a man-for-man basis. After he leaves that area, the zone men should be able to pick him up with little trouble. When he is in the shaded area, the four zone men are constantly helping the middle man prevent passes to the pivot area.

These defenses are especially good against teams that use static offenses against zone defenses. Show them the 1-3-1 zone formation when they come down the floor. Entice them to set up their offense in the formation most familiar to your team. In a sense, you are hiding the zone-and-one defense until the offense gets near the scoring area. Then let the defensive player who drew the man-for-man assignment begin his harrassment. If he is guarding a pivot man, chances are that it will take a while before the offense discovers they are facing something other than a 1-3-1 zone.

Factors to Consider in Installing the Zone-and-One

The zone-and-one variations can be incorporated into your defensive approach without spending endless hours trying to perfect them. However, before deciding to use one of these defenses, several things need to be considered.

Is the man you wish to double up on dangerous enough to warrant the use of a zone-and-one? Evaluate his special talents.

Check his shooting percentage for the season to see how consistent he is. Does he rebound on the offensive boards? When some players are screened away from the boards, their point production drops sharply.

What about the other four men on offense? Is the zone strong enough to stop them? Do not weaken your defense on the other four just to stop one. There have been occasions when the defense has been keyed to stop one player; and although this purpose was accomplished, the other four players scored easy buckets to win the game. Stopping a key player does not always open the door to victory.

ZONE-AND-TWO

Occasionally, there will be a team whose offensive strength is shouldered completely by two players. Such a situation is more likely to exist in high school than college. It is easier for high school boys to dominate their team's offense. In college it is more likely that the clever execution of an offensive pattern will

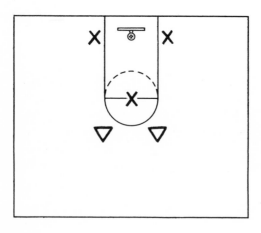

Diagram 35

result in the use of a combination defense. Whatever the reason, the three-man zone with two men guarding assigned men can be utilized effectively in some situations.

Setting Up the Zone-and-Two

The zone-and-two, or triangle-and-two, can be set up in two ways. The triangle can be created by the zone play of the three deep or baseline men. The two front men play their men all over the halfcourt, using man-for-man tactics. (See Diagram 35.)

Once again, the basic zone principles as applied in the 1-3-1 are used so that this is not a complete new learning situation. Since X5 normally flexes to his left and X2 drops back to position opposite X5, there is no difficulty establishing the two-man base of the triangle. The middle man (X3) simply retains his position on the free-throw line to form the point of the triangle. The other two men are left for the man-for-man assignments. (See Diagrams 36 and 37.)

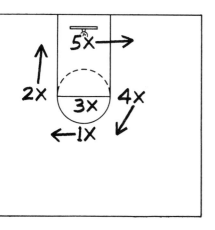

Diagram 36

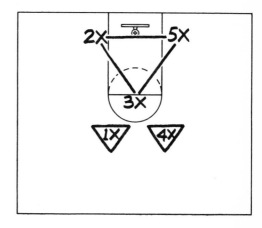

Diagram 37

The three men forming the triangle zone cover these positions when the ball goes to the corner. (See Diagrams 38 and 39.)

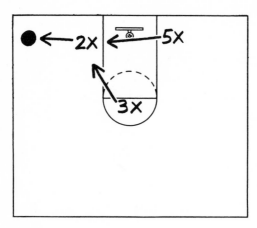

Diagram 38

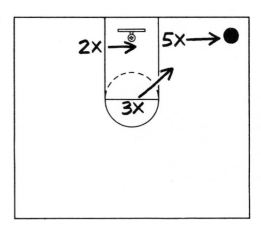

Diagram 39

The three deep men react differently when the ball is in the area of the free-throw line extended. (See Diagrams 40 and 41.)

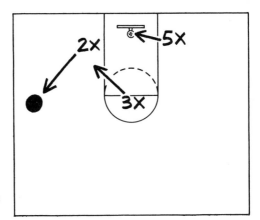

Diagram 40

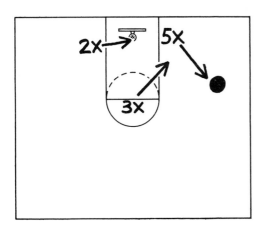

Diagram 41

Try to keep the offense from recognizing the zone-and-two. Cover it up by sending the two front men out to harass the guards as they cross centerline. Have the other three men stand near the offensive player in their area. This will present the appearance of a man-for-man defense. When the ball penetrates the frontcourt area, the three men forming the triangle can drop off to their zone.

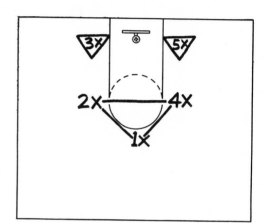

Diagram 42

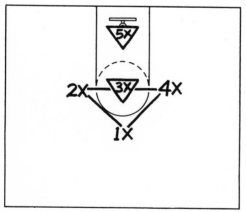

Diagram 43

Against a team whose chief threats are the forwards, the triangle can be set another way. The idea now is to enclose the top half of the circle with the three-man zone, and assign man-for-man defense to the two deep men. This defense is particularly strong against teams with two big men who are used on the high and low post areas or as a double post combination. Diagrams 42 and 43 show the way the defense sets up.

X3 and X5 guard their men on a man-for-man basis. They stay with them wherever they go.

Zone and Two Dangerous against 1-3-1 and 3-2

Restrict the use of this defense against 1-3-1 and 3-2 offenses. Overloads can be mighty dangerous against either of the zone-and-two defenses. Sometimes it is necessary to show the offense one defense as they come down the floor, so the offense will attack with the appropriate formation. Most teams will usually attack a 2-1-2 zone with a 1-3-1 or a 3-2 formation. Here is a good opportunity to lure the offense into your trap. Show them a 2-1-2 zone when they come down the floor. As they set up their offensive formation, move into the triangle zone and pick up the two pivot men.

The two defenders who guard the deep men have a job that is vital to the over-all success of the defense. Since post men are usually top rebounding threats, they must be kept away from the boards after a shot. Screening post men away from the boards is no easy task, since the defense should be fronting the offensive post men slightly to prevent passes to him. If these two defenders can also eliminate tap-ins, they will be as valuable in a rebounding capacity as in a defender's role.

The zone-and-two defenses actually employ one of the following principles—zone the guards and play the deep men (forwards and pivot) man-for-man, or man-for-man the guards and zone the back men. These defenses work better when scouting information reveals a distinct weakness at both guard positions or both forward positions. Such weaknesses can be capitalized on by zoning and allowing the zone men to drop off and protect against some other strength.

THE TANDEM-AND-THREE

Here is an appropriate defense to be used against a team with one outstanding guard. The defense takes its name from the "stacked" position of the two guards. The other three defenders station themselves in a baseline zone. (See Diagram 44.)

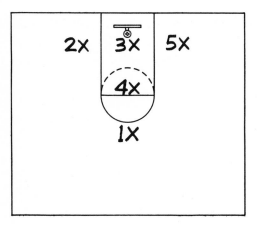

Diagram 44

The top defender (X1) on the tandem comes out and plays the most dangerous offensive guard as long as he remains at the guard position. (See Diagram 45.) When the guard goes to the corner the entire defense becomes a zone. (See Diagrams 46 and 47.)

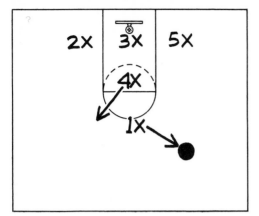

Diagram 45

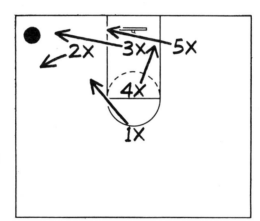

Diagram 46

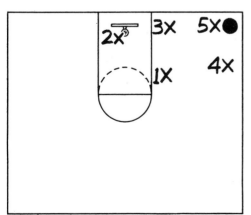

Diagram 47

The entire team reacts to the zone as if they were playing the 1-3-1. X3 covers the left corner and X5 covers the right corner. The slides are kept the same for simplicity. It may be necessary against teams with an outstanding corner threat to let X2 pick up in the corner until 3X arrives, but other than this there is little need to deviate from the basic movement of the 1-3-1.

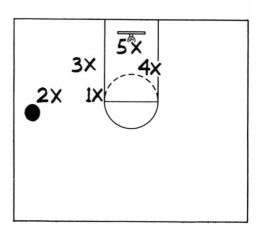

Diagram 48

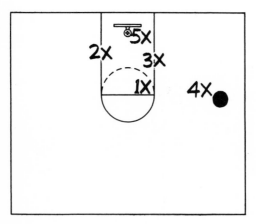

Diagram 49

Diagrams 48 and 49 show the way the defense covers when the ball is at the wing position.

The tandem-and-three will also work well against a team that does not have an outstanding pivot threat.

6

Stunting with Pressure Defenses

Stunting with pressure-type defenses is a good way to destroy a team's confidence. Sometimes, I feel the term "pressure defense" is a misnomer, because any defense that does not place pressure on the offense will not be effective. Defense is not passive; however, the term "pressure defense" in modern basketball vernacular refers to defenses designed to harass and double-team the offense. Halfcourt, three-quarter court and fullcourt presses provide double-team situations and backcourt harassment. These defenses prevent the offense from relaxing and keep them guessing, expecting the worse. When the offense is subjected to such constant harassment, mistakes are made.

Pressure defenses have changed the game about as much as the jump shot. They have helped to take the play away from the big boy by forcing a wide-open type of play where speed and aggressiveness can be utilized.

THE 1-3-1 ZONE PRESS

In keeping with the theory of the flexing zone, we like to use the basic 1-3-1 zone defense and simply move it out to cover more area. The defensive players can be moved out to a half-court, three-quarter, or fullcourt basis. We seldom use a fullcourt press, since it spreads the defense too much and permits easy penetration passes. The halfcourt press and three-quarter zone press produce as well, yet the gamble is not as great.

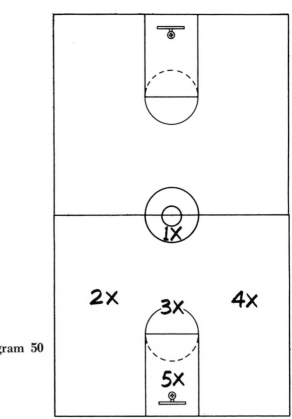

Diagram 50

Diagrams 50, 51, and 52 show the starting positions for each
of the presses. The matching principle is once again employed
since a defensive player is useless guarding an area of the floor
that is unoccupied. On the press, the defensive players must rely
heavily on peripheral vision to pick up offensive players as they
move from one spot on the court to another.

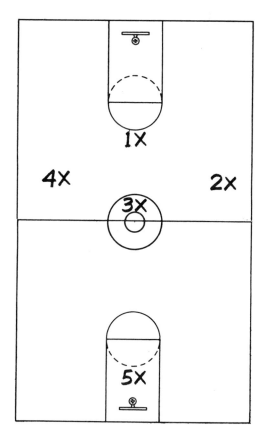

Diagram 51

The point man (X1) has the most important job on the zone press. He should not contest the throw in. Have the point man guide the dribbler to a position on the sideline where you would like the double-team to be made. If the fullcourt press is used, pick up the dribbler as soon as he receives the in-bounds pass.

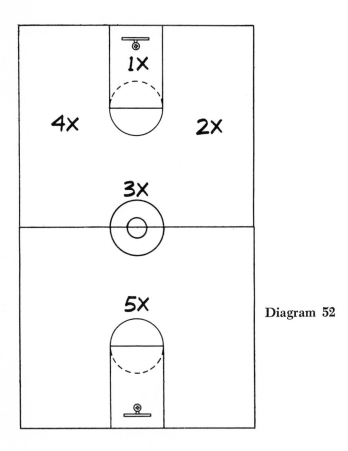

Diagram 52

On the three-quarter court press, pick up in the area of the free-throw line. When the halfcourt press is used, let the point man apply his pressure just as the dribbler approaches the half-court line.

Location of the Double Teaming

There are many theories as to where the double-team should

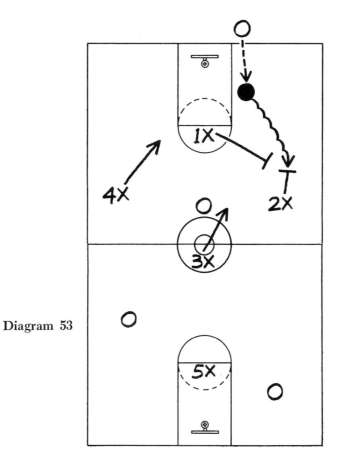

Diagram 53

be applied. Some teams try to force the double-team as soon as possible without consideration to court position. Others like to lure the dribbler away from the trailing official. Despite the advantages offered by these choices, we have found, particularly in high school, that the double-team is more effective when the dribbler is forced to use his "weak hand." Since this is the left

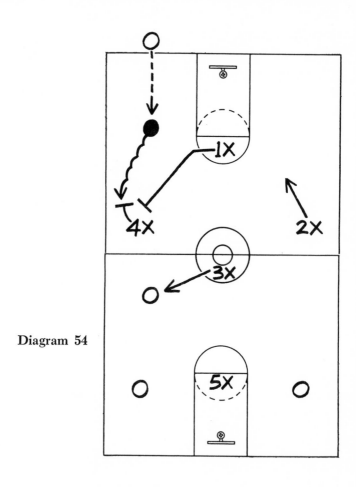

Diagram 54

hand in most cases, instruct the point man to drive the dribbler toward X2 by overplaying the dribbler's strong hand and encouraging him to use his "weak hand." At a point near the sideline, the double-team is made. Diagram 53 shows where the double-team is applied on the three-quarter court press.

As X2 and X1 converge to make the double-team, the other three players react and move, looking for the interception. The middle man (X3) plugs the middle. X4 covers the weak-side of the floor and prevents a quick pass back to the offensive player who passed the ball in bounds. If there is no one in the middle, X3 should drop back and play for the interception to either side of the court. The goalie (X5) protects the goal on any penetration beyond the frontline of defenders.

Should the ball be dribbled to the other side of the floor, X4 becomes the double-teamer, X2 the interceptor. X3 has the same responsibilities. X5 always protects the basket and should not gamble on an interception unless he is 100 per cent sure he will be able to make the steal.

THE HALFCOURT PRESS

Missed field goal and free-throw attempts make it difficult to set up a three-quarter or fullcourt zone press. Quick outlet passes eliminate the double-team opportunities. To prevent cheap baskets, fall back into a halfcourt press when possession of the ball is changed by any situation other than the scoring of a field goal or free throw. Use this same defense when the offense escapes the backcourt trap and advances the ball into the frontcourt against either the three-quarter court press or fullcourt press. The halfcourt press also makes a good defense to use separately. It provides ample opportunity to double-team and intercept, yet remains compact enough to prevent easy baskets.

The initial alignment of players is the same as in the 1-3-1 zone; however, different slides are used to set up the double-team. Once again, the point man has the all-important job of

encouraging the dribbler to use his weak hand. The trap with
the double-team ideally should take place just as the ball crosses

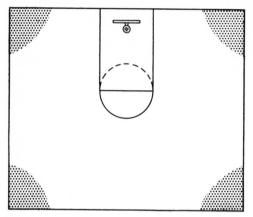

Diagram 55

centerline. Mistakes are more likely when the ball-handler not
only has to worry about the double-team, but also the 10-second

Diagram 56

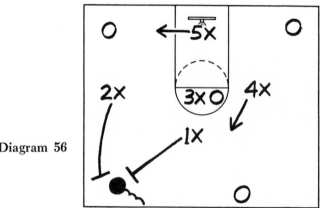

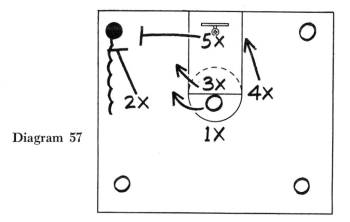

Diagram 57

line. If the double-team is timed correctly, the midcourt line
and sideline will serve as defensive men as well and actually

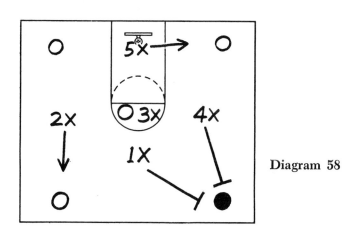

Diagram 58

result in a quarter-team. Sometimes, the dribbler will escape the
first double-team. When this happens, force the dribbler to the

corner. The shaded areas in diagram 55 represent the best places
to double-team. See diagrams 56 through 59 for double-team
situations.

Diagram 59

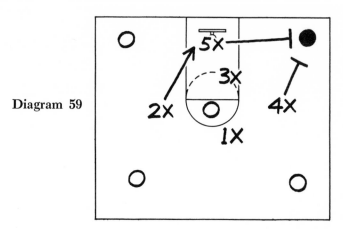

When employing the halfcourt press, a most important point
of execution is for the wing men to drop to the goal when the

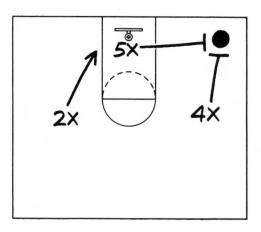

Diagram 60

ball is in the opposite corner. The goalie must leave the critical scoring area when the ball goes to the corner. He double-teams with the strong-side wing man. (See Diagram 60.)

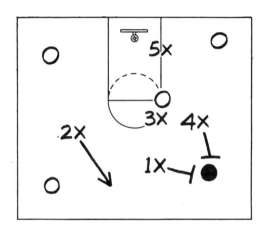

Diagram 61

When the ball is between the free-throw line extended and centercourt, the off-side wing man is an interceptor, but as soon as the ball passes the free-throw line extended, he drops off as rapidly as possible to cover the goal area that X5 has evacuated.

Diagram 61 shows X2's position as an off-side interceptor when the ball is in the frontcourt.

DRILLS FOR PERFECTING THE PRESS

The secret of the zone press is the double-team. Instruct your players not to be overanxious. The players who make the double-team seldom steal the ball. They should concentrate on an aggressive double-team without fouling and close off any escape outlet the ball-handler may have. If the players making the double-team can force a lob pass or some other offensive error, then their part on the press has been executed perfectly.

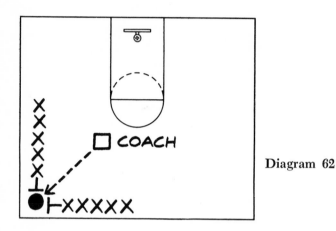

Diagram 62

Again I emphasize—do not commit petty, unnecessary fouls by impatiently overguarding.

Since the double-team and interception are the heart and soul of any zone press, spend a great deal of time in practice drilling your players on these maneuvers. A number of simple drills can be devised to practice the double-team and interception. We have used some that have produced outstanding results.

Practice the double-team by placing one player near the sideline. (See Diagram 62.) Form two lines of defensive double-teamers on each side of him. Throw the ball to the offensive player and have the defensive players converge, using a wide base and arms spread. Give everyone a chance to practice the double-team from various spots on the floor. Continually emphasize the importance of harassment without fouling. Occasionally, time the defensive players to see how long they can

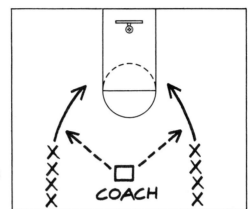

Diagram 63

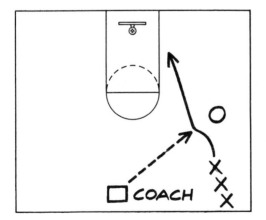

Diagram 64

contain the ball-handler without fouling or allowing him to free himself.

Catching the ball cleanly on the interception and converting the steal into a basket is not an easy chore. Break down this phase of your zone press and work on it also. Instead of warming up with the conventional two-line lay-up drill, have the players breaking to meet passes or picking up rolling passes off the floor. (See Diagram 63.) You might station one player at a particular spot and pass to him. Improve the timing of your players and make them interception-minded by having them break in front of the offensive player and take the pass. (See Diagram 64.) After the interception is made, have the offensive player chase the interceptor to the basket, placing some pressure on the lay-up as would exist under actual game conditions. These "catch-and-go" drills will have a carry-over to offensive ball-handling as well.

Combine the Drills

After these drills have been worked on separately, combine

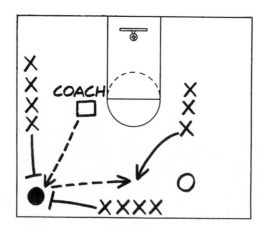

Diagram 65

them. Have the ball-handler attempt to pass to a teammate while he is being double-teamed. Let part of the players work on timing the interception while others practice the double-team. Move the drill to different places on the floor, so your players will become familiar with all double-team and interception situations. (See Diagram 65.) These drills will improve any zone press designed to trap the ball-handler and intercept his pass.

PLACEMENT OF PERSONNEL

Positioning of personnel is one key to the success of any zone press. On the 1-3-1, place the slowest player under the goal. Tell him to guard the area under the basket when the

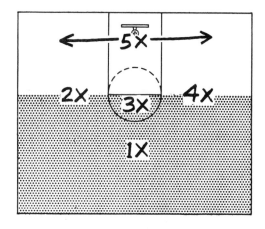

Diagram 66

ball is between centerline and the free-throw line extended.

(See shaded area in Diagram 66.) When the ball moves into either corner, he moves out to double-team.

Wingmen

The two wing men (X2 and X4) should have good speed and sure hands, since they make most of the interceptions. It is

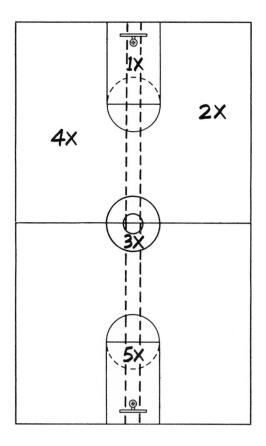

Diagram 67

better to have men with some height advantage at these positions, because the added height will make the double-team more effective and aid in making interceptions.

Generally, we divide the court in half by drawing an imaginary line from one basket to the other. (See Diagram 67.) Then we tell each wing man to double-team with either the point man or goalie when the ball is in this area. Of course, this seems like an extremely large area for one man to cover, but if the wing man will wait until the point man drives the dribbler to him, he will find his job much easier. He should not come to meet the dribbler but should let the point man force him to the sidelines. If a good job is done on the first double-team, there will be little concern over the large area to the back of the wing men. If the dribbler escapes the double-team, the wing man must aid in driving the ball back to the sidelines so a new double team situation can be set up.

By looking at Diagram 67, it is easy to see why we favor the three-quarter and halfcourt press. We teach the halfcourt press first, then move it out to cover more area when the situation demands.

Middle Man

The middle man (X3) is usually one of the tallest men on the squad whose mobility is somewhat lacking. He should be a good rebounder. His primary responsibility is to plug the middle and discourage passes to that area. He is also responsible for picking up dribblers who escape the double-team and drive for the basket. It is difficult to designate a particular area for this man, since much of his work is free-lance. However, like the goalie (X5), he should not be too anxious to intercept and leave the middle open. Diagram 68 shows the general area of responsibility for the middle man.

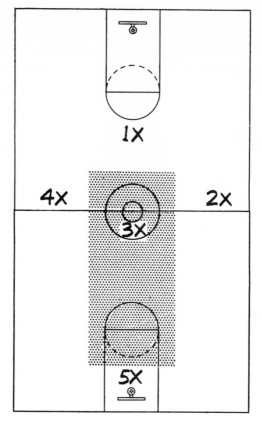

Diagram 68

Point Position

Usually, the point position is reserved for the fastest and best defensive player on the team. One of the guards ordinarily fill this position well. However, simple logic tells us it is best to place a fairly tall player at this position. A short point man will allow the offense to pass the ball over his outstretched arms. Therefore, it is sensible to sacrifice a little speed for size at this position, especially on the halfcourt press.

Upon seeing our halfcourt press shackled by one team because we placed our shortest players at the point position and the two wings, we decided to make some changes. The opposing team had spread out and tossed the ball back and forth at centerline, with our mighty mites peering at their belt buckles. The opponents spent the latter part of the game playing "keep away" from our defense. Later on in the season when we met the team again, we pulled our biggest boy from the goalie position and moved him to the point and placed our 5'9" point man under the goal. The strategy paid off handsomely. The bigger point man caused more errant passes and we won the game when one of our wing men moved up and intercepted a lob that some 5'10" guard had tried to pass over our 6'2" point man.

Other high school teams in this area have made similar personnel adjustments. There seems to be a growing tendency to place the tallest men on the frontline of the zone press, and to let the shortest, fastest play under the basket. Coaches who are using this idea feel that the short, fast men can get back down the floor faster and protect against the fast-break. The bigger, slower men can execute the double-team better, since their body spread covers more area. Because the big men in basketball are becoming increasingly mobile and agile, this change of personnel placement on the zone press may affect everyone on all levels before long.

ALTERNATIONS WITH THE ZONE PRESS

Using the cues that have already been described in Chapter 4, a number of different alterations can be derived from pressure defenses.

Switching to the Fullcourt Man-for-Man

One of the best ways to alternate pressure defenses is to change from a three-quarter court zone press to a fullcourt man-for-man press. It is inadvisable to be labeled strictly a zone press team, since most teams have now found methods to attack the zone press and destroy its effectiveness. Possessing a strong man-for-man press will give you another weapon in your defensive arsenal, as well as make the advantages of alternating defenses available to you. Having only one press eliminates the surprise.

Alternating the three-quarter court zone press with the fullcourt man-for-man press offsets the offensive strategy of clearing and letting one man advance the ball across midcourt. The objective would be to catch the dribbler in the backcourt and double-team him before he could receive any help from his teammates who cleared because they thought they were facing a man-for-man press. The clear-out can be encouraged by using the man-for-man press several times and quickly changing to a zone press.

Because the game situation in which the press is used is usually tense, you would probably do better to make the change at a time out. However, if the press is used as a part of the overall game plan and not just in the closing stages of the game, then the alteration can be made by a defensive quarterback or through the use of another signal.

Stunts with the Press

Stunts with the press can be successfully utilized with your normal halfcourt defenses. Use the scoreboard as a cue. When the opponent's score is an odd number, move your defense out and pick up the offense somewhere in the backcourt. Occasional pressure will shake their confidence and keep them from relaxing.

The halfcourt zone press and the regular 1-3-1 zone make a perfect combination for alternating defenses. Since both start from the same basic formation, it is easier to deceive the offense and surprise them with a quick double team. The point man can determine when to make the change by using hand signals or positioning himself at a specific spot on the floor.

A clenched fist held behind the point man's back can be the signal for the halfcourt press. One finger extended means that the normal 1-3-1 flexing zone will be used. If the opposing team catches these signals, a different set of signals can be employed at a time out without breaking the defensive pattern. Indicate the change to the press by having the point man take his first position inside the center circle as the offense comes down the floor. When he stations himself near the front of the foul circle, use the normal 1-3-1 zone. These same signals can be used in changing from normal halfcourt to three-quarter and fullcourt presses.

When using a defensive quarterback to change defenses, it is important that he be an offensive safety man. He should be the first person downcourt so he can signal the defense as the other players assume their defensive positions.

CONCEALED ZONE PRESS

Some teams have developed their pressing defense to the point that it is impossible to tell whether it is a zone or man-for-man press. In a sense, they conceal their zone press by guarding each offensive player man-for-man until a situation arises when a trap or double-team can be made.

We are in the experimental stage with such a defense, and

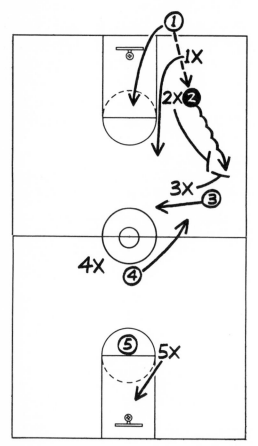

Diagram 69

in talking with other coaches who use this defense, they seem to be also. This press operates better on a fullcourt basis. Its success depends on the ability of the defensive player guarding the ball to force the dribbler into a congested area, preferably along the sidelines, where a teammate can leave his man and double-team. The player nearest the ball leaves his man to help make the trap. When the trap is made, the other three defensive players zone the area that they occupy and look for the interception. If the double-team is broken or the interception is missed, every defensive player returns to his assigned man until another double-team situation results.

In Diagram 69, X2 has driven O2 to the sideline. X3 leaves his man and double-teams, because he is the defensive player nearest the ball and his assigned man has cut away from the ball. X4 zones the area around the centercourt and looks for the interception on the pass to O3. The defensive reactions would be the same if O3 had cut down the sidelines to the basket, except that X4 would drop back and zone the sideline area.

Of course, if no double-team is made, then the defense is in a normal man-for-man press. Cooperation and willingness to pick up loose men make or break this defense. The only way to perfect it is through constant drill until each player knows and senses the time to leave his man and double-team. The double-team need not be made on the sidelines. It can be made on offensive crosses involving screens and hand-offs or short shovel passes.

When using this press, we have found the following to be ideal situations in which to double-team:

1. When there is a cross of two offensive players involving the ball.
2. When an offensive man cuts away from the ball, leaving his defensive man nearest the defensive player guarding the ball.

3. When an offensive man is driven to the corner. Defensive
man nearest the ball double-teams.

ZONE-AND-ONE ZONE PRESS

When you face a team that has built its offense around one
player, the zone-and-one zone press can solve your problem of

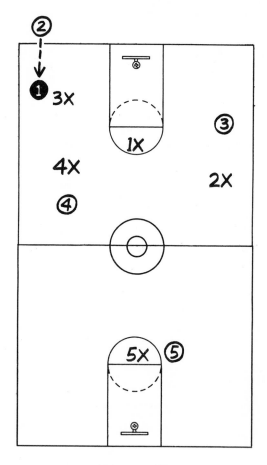

Diagram 70

stopping the high-scoring phenom. It enables the defense to pressure one player, yet capitalize on poor passing and dribbling by the other four players.

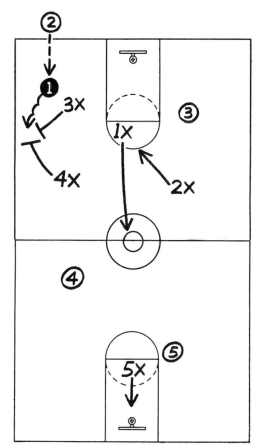

Diagram 71

As mentioned previously, it is best to try to stop the really good boy without changing too many of your established defensive habits. By using the 1-3-1 halfcourt, three-quarter, or fullcourt zone press, the middle man can be assigned to guard the superstar on a man-for-man basis. His primary purpose is to keep the assigned man from getting the ball.

There is a definite weakness created in the middle, but in order to gain an advantage there will, of necessity, be a weakness elsewhere. The two wing men can pinch toward the middle slightly to help protect that area. Otherwise, all moves and slides are the same as with the 1-3-1 press. The zone now depends on only four men to double-team and intercept instead of five. The diamond formation is the same as the zone-and-one defense described earlier.

In Diagram 70, X3 is guarding O1 on a man-for-man basis, while the other four players have assumed their normal positions on the three-quarter zone press. X3 must overplay O1 and keep him from receiving a pass. Should O1 receive a pass, then X3 must force him to the sideline, where the wing man on that side (X4) will help make the trap. The point man (X1) should drop to the middle, since X3 has assumed his responsibility of directing the dribbler to the sidelines for the double-team. X2 plays for the interception and X5 protects the basket. (See Diagram 71.)

When O1 gets rid of the ball, X1 then assumes his regular duties as point man and picks up the dribbler trying to lure him into the trap.

SUMMARY

Pressure defenses lay claim to the spectacular. No basketball team can afford to be without some variation of a pressure defense, because basketball is a game that reaches out for the most spectacular achievements in the athletic world. No team can ever be counted out of a game as long as it can put that extra effort into perfecting its pressure defense.

Here are some of the teaching pointers requiring special emphasis in stunting with pressure defenses:

1. Sell your players on the value of pressure defenses.
2. Get set before the ball is put in play. Each player should know where his position is and go there immediately.
3. Encourage the offense to dribble, then force the dribbler to the sidelines before making the double-team.
4. Keep the ball away from the middle of the floor.
5. Make sure there is always one safety man to protect against snowbirds.
6. Force the offense to use the lob pass or the bounce pass. These are the slowest passes and are easily intercepted.
7. Break your pressure defenses down and work on the double-team and interception separately.
8. Teach the halfcourt zone press first. Then move it out to cover more area, using the same slides.

7

Concealed Defenses

Some offenses render the personnel of a particular team less effective than others. For this reason, it is a good idea to try to force the offense into using an offensive attack that is least likely to present a scoring hazard. Occasionally, you will find certain offenses easier to cover. In these situations, conceal the actual defense until the offense begins to make their approach. As soon as the offense recognizes the initial defense, have your players move into the actual defense either on a prearranged cue or automatically.

Teams with a zone defense and a man-for-man defense can use concealment. By showing a zone defense as the offense approaches and then quickly picking up man-for-man assignments, it is likely that you will catch the offense attacking your man-for-man defense with their zone offense. Since zone defenses usually do not involve screens and a large number of cutters, this could be an advantage.

The reverse can also be used. The zone can be concealed by having your players act as if they are picking up their man-for-man assignments as the offense comes down the floor. Tell them to fake the man-for-man defense, verbally disillusioning the offense. Calling, "I've got fourteen. Pick up your man tight," will help to convince the offense you really are playing man-for-man defense.

When the offense crosses the 10-second line, the defense can begin to move into its zone positions. It is best to use a zone formation that blends well with the offensive formation. Better still, apply the rules of the flexing zone and be prepared to meet any offensive alignment.

DRAW YOUR OPPONENTS INTO THEIR WEAKEST OFFENSE

Similarly, two different types of zone defenses may be employed. If your scouting report shows a zone offense with a definite weakness, set up the zone defense that will entice the opponents to use their weakest offense. For example, suppose Central High always attacked a 2-1-2 zone with a 1-3-1 static offense. The scouting report on Central showed their wing men

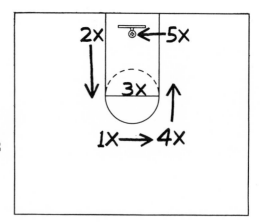

Diagram 72

to be weak, long-range shooters. Because of the inability of their wing men to score from outside, the 1-3-1 offense should not be too effective. By showing a 2-1-2 zone as the offense comes down the floor, the 1-3-1 offense would be used and the 2-1-2 zone could be flexed to cover the offense.

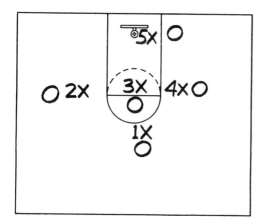

Diagram 73

The flex would be accomplished by reversing the match-ups in Diagram 14. Each defensive player would move to cover the offensive threats in different areas, so that the defense now resembled a 1-3-1 zone. (See Diagrams 72 and 73.)

USE CONCEALMENT SPARINGLY

It is unlikely that concealment will be useful throughout the entire course of the game. It may only work for three or four minutes during the crucial part of the game. These few minutes may be just enough to turn the tide in a close game.

On the other hand, the confusion created by the bedlam and noise of a game often makes the players and coaches the least reliable people to determine the type of defense their opponents are using. Points lost while experimenting with inappropriate offenses can pave the way to defeat.

CONCEALING A FLEXING ZONE

An excellent way to conceal a flexing zone is to have your defensive guards move out and press the offensive guards at centerline or further. The pressure can be applied three-quartercourt, fullcourt, or halfcourt, but as soon as the offense approaches the scoring area, have the two guards drop off into their normal flexing zone positions. This backcourt harassment in itself will be an effective weapon. Chances are, the offense will be so disgruntled when first faced with the pressure, they will not question the possibility of being confronted with a zone defense.

CONCEALING A MAN-FOR-MAN

One way to conceal a man-for-man defense is to set up a three-man front, as is the case with the zone press. Double-team the first pass in bounds and play for the interception on the next pass. If the double-team and interception attempt are unsuccessful, drop back quickly down the floor and pick up the assigned men. Such a defense would work only on out-of-bounds situations. On all other turnovers, the defense would merely sprint down the floor and defend on a man-for-man basis.

Some offenses begin with a basic 2-1-2 floor balance, but after sending a cutter through, the basic balance becomes a

1-3-1 formation. Continuity may or may not be obtained from this point.

Play the initial formation man-for-man. Follow the cutter, in most cases a guard, through to the baseline and defend from the normal 1-3-1 zone at that point. This defense can be used against the shuffle offense. (See Diagram 74.)

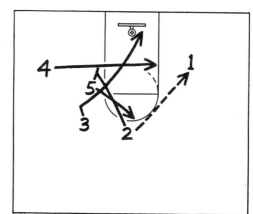

Diagram 74

Diagram 75 shows how the man-for-man defense would be aligned with the offense. After X3 followed the cutter through to the baseline, the 1-3-1 defense would resemble that shown in Diagram 76.

To execute this defense, both guards should know how to play both the point position and the goalie position, since each would be forced to play the positions, depending on whose man went through as a cutter.

The shuffle is versatile enough to prevent such a simple plan from working over a sustained period of time. The ball can be thrown in to the number 4 man or the number 5 man.

A pass to either of these men could be the cue for a 2-1-2 zone.
This might confuse your own players, however, and the
simplest procedure would be to use the man-for-man at all
times except when the ball is passed to number 1. This would
be the cue to follow the cutter and defend from the 1-3-1 zone.

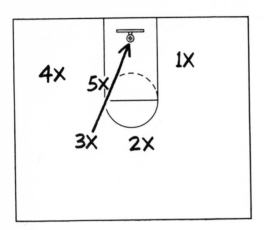

Diagram 75

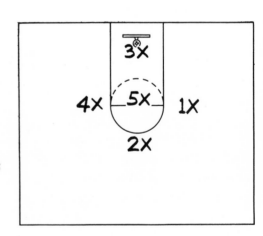

Diagram 76

SUMMARY

There are countless ways to effect defensive concealment. Your own ingenuity can produce many different ways to cover or hide a particular defense. Attacking with the wrong offense can be a frustrating and demoralizing situation to the opposing coach, as well as his team.

Remember, the concealment may not be effective for long. When the offense catches on, change to something different.

8

Strong-Side Combination Defense

There are as many stunting defenses as there are basketball coaches in America. We cannot resist the temptation to play chess with our players. As often as not, these stunts backfire. Stunting can be very dangerous.

A good time to stunt is when you feel you have nothing to lose. A stunting defense might catch a stronger opponent off guard. If you can create confusion and insecurity in the opposition's offense, the stunting defense can be a great equalizer. Of course, we feel defense *is* the great equalizer in basketball. In football, a muddy field may bring an extremely strong team and an extremely weak team closer to each other in ability on a given night.

USE AGAINST A TEAM WITH A SET PATTERN

Stunting defenses are notoriously effective against strongly set, mechanical pattern teams. When you can safely predict the routes each player will take during most of the game, you should be able to do something to make these routes less effective.

A stunting defense might even come in handy on a night when you are the favorite and find yourself on the losing end of the score. This would be in keeping with the old coach's axiom, "Do *something,* even if it's wrong." In other words, don't just sit around and let the game get away when some adjustment could be made. Even if it is wrong, you will have the satisfaction of knowing that something is being done. Of course, a stunting defense may not be the appropriate action. Substitutions, offensive adjustments, and other adjustments might be more appropriate.

BEST TIMES TO STUNT

So a stunting defense may well be used when:

1. you have everything to gain and nothing to lose (the opposition is much too strong for you);
2. against pattern teams that are too mechanical; or
3. when you find yourself on the losing end of the score in any game.

A fourth possibility could be based on a simple test of your opposition. Test them in the first two or three plays to see if they know what to do with a stunting defense. If they do, change on a prearranged signal to a simpler defense. If they do not know what to do with stunting defenses, stay in the defense as long as it is effective.

We have all seen the great upset, the shocking loss by a powerful team to a so-called small, weak one. Sometimes we read about it and sometimes we hear through friends about such an upset. Keep a file giving the reasons for such upsets over the next ten years, and you will find that 90 per cent of them are the result of a stunting defense used by the underdog.

ALL COACHES USE STUNTS

Many coaches use stunting defenses without realizing it. Quite often you flex a zone or adjust a man-to-man to create a stunting defense as the game progresses. When you have an offside guard or an offside foward "fronting" a post man while your defending post man plays normally, this is certainly a stunting defense. "Sandwiching" the big man is almost as old as the game. If you automatically double-team in the corners, you are a stunting defensive coach. If you zone an opponent and simply allow their very weak fifth man to roam free while you concentrate your five on their remaining four, you are stunting. The day has nearly passed when a team will use what we consider a straight, normal zone or a regular man-to-man.

We would certainly agree that it is far better to perfect one defense than to use several in a ragged, haphazard manner. It is also foolhardy to out-coach yourself in a burst of genius with last-minute stunts that confuse your own boys. We must always teach the fundamentals first and teach them well. We must build our defensive teams on a firm foundation.

THE ORIGIN OF THE STRONG-SIDE COMBINATION

The defense we will now discuss is called "strong-side combination" because we use the words "strong side" and "weak side." The defense was devised by a high school coach in Alabama. He wrote asking help in working out a clear definition of this defense. He was also very apologetic and said that his boys were sometimes confused, but he explained that the opposition was even more confused. I thought it was one of the best new ideas I had heard and told him not to apologize for such a fine, original defense. One of the beauties of this defense is that the opposition has a very hard time defining it. Sometimes, it appears to be a combination baseline zone and man-to-man on the guards. Other times, it appears to be a zone, and on still other occasions it appears to be a man-to-man. It is none of these, and at times it is all of them.

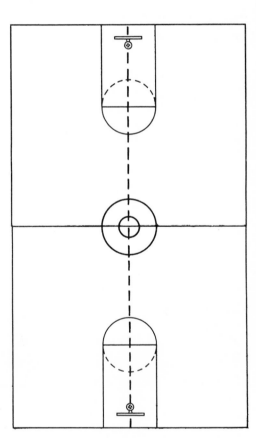

Diagram 77

DIVIDE THE COURT IN HALF LENGTHWISE

The court is divided into halves, but not the halves we normally think about. Draw a line midway down the floor from one basket to the other. Teach your boys to think of the court in vertical halves. The half or side of the floor the ball is on represents the strong side. The other half represents the weak side. (See Diagram 77.)

Be sure the boys have a clear mental picture of the strong and weak side, with the halves of the floor from goal to goal vividly in mind. Your baseline will be defensed by zone tactics at all times. (See Diagram 78.) Your three front men—the two

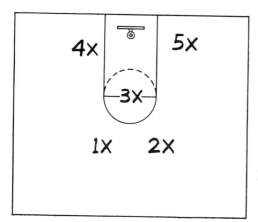

Diagram 78

forwards and center—handle this. The two guards will play man-to-man until the offensive guards penetrate the scoring zone. At this point, your guards have to react quickly to initiate the strong-side combination defense.

Each guard will play his man-to-man *when* his opponent is on the strong side, whether he has the ball or not. When his opponent is on that side of the floor represented by the strong side, with or without the ball, the guard will play his man, using good man-to-man tactics. (See Diagram 79.) *When* his opponent leaves the strong side and goes to the other side, away from the ball, which we have designated as the weak side, he will zone and his position will be determined by the location of the ball. (See Diagram 80.) Most of the time he should stand on the imaginary line from goal to goal, directly in line with the ball and his opponent, so that he can pick up his opponent quickly if that man should come into the strong-side area.

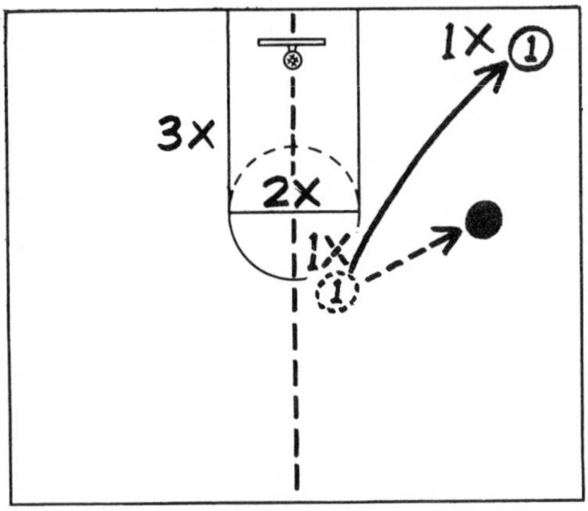

Diagram 79

DEFENSIVE SLIDES

The defensive slides for the three front men who are zoning are the same as if they were playing a 2-1-2 defense. (See

MAN AWAY FROM BALL

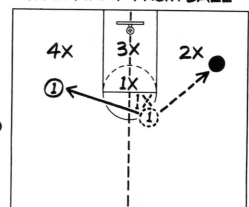

Diagram 80

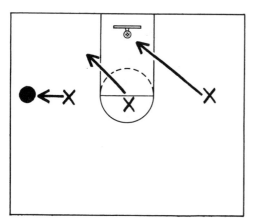

Diagram 81

Diagrams 81 and 82.) Subtle differences will crop up when
a guard is playing his opponent man-to-man in the vicinity
of a zoning player. In an initial set-up, these three men will
match up with any opponent in their area. They move as

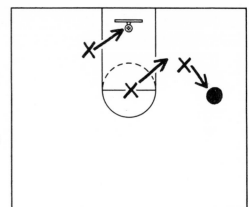

Diagram 82

soon as the player moves. Many variations will occur, but they have only two widely varying formations to defend. Both of these are corner situations. Their slides will be quite different

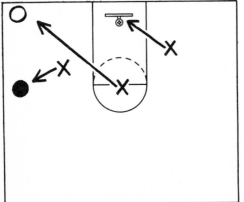

Diagram 83

if there is an offensive wing man and an offensive corner man, neither of whom is being played man-to-man by a guard. (See Diagrams 83 and 84.) They must categorize these formations

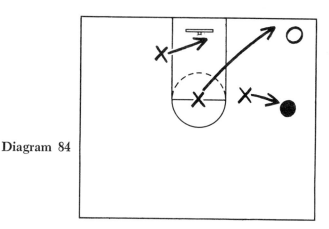

Diagram 84

as one man in the corner or two men in the corner. When there is only one man in the corner, he is obviously defended by the forward on that wing.

RULES OF PLAY

So the rules are very simple:

1. All front men—zone the baseline.
2. Strong-side guard—play man-to-man.
3. Weak-side guard—zone.

Of course, the guards must be able to adjust quickly from zone to man-to-man. This one facet of the defense prevents it from being too simple. The frontline men cannot afford simply to stand like store-window dummies. Their slides should be carefully worked out and clearly defined. All players will operate at all times on the sound defensive axiom, "Don't waste yourself." This means that even the guard who is playing man-to-man will not go out to centercourt and press his strong-side opponent while his opponent is out of scoring contention. This means that the weak-side zoning guard contributes to the total defense while he is zoning.

APPLY THE RULES TO THE OPPONENTS' PLAYS

If you will take these rules and apply them to several of your opponents' patterns or offensive plays, you will see that the defense appears to change almost at random, and is extremely difficult to define. At one point you are in a 1-4, with one man playing man-to-man and four zoning. (Diagram 85.) At one

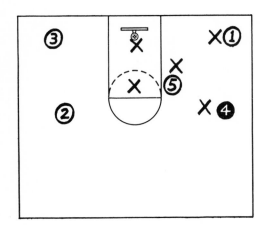

Diagram 85

point you are in a 2-3 (see Diagram 86), with two men playing man-to-man and three zoning. On another occasion, everybody appears to be zoning. (See Diagram 87.)

Let us take two patterns and run through them completely, utilizing the rules that we have listed. Of course, the teams that use these patterns do not stand still so nicely and may have adjustments of their own. However, let us walk through the Drake Shuffle utilizing the strong-side combination defense.

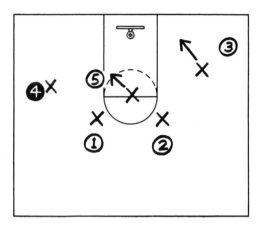

Diagram 86

Diagram 87
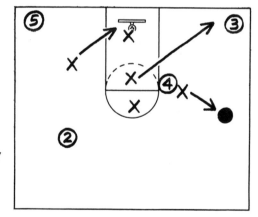

The Drake Shuffle

First of all, we play man-to-man until the guards get into their normal set-up in the scoring zone. The three baseline men should match up to the nearest offensive player in the area to make it appear to be all man-to-man. At this point, we have both guards in the strong side, or the side of the ball, since O3 usually starts the pattern. Both guards are playing man-to-man. (See Diagram 88.)

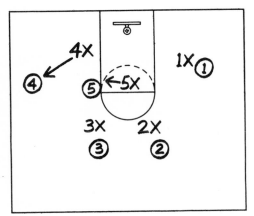

Diagram 88

O3 passes to O2, and O2 to O1. The guard (3X) on O3 is playing a cutter moving to the strong-side man, so he is playing man-to-man, as is the other guard (2X). The baseline cut by O4 is ineffective because the deep men (1X, 5X, 4X) are still zoning. (See Diagram 89.)

On the interchange between O2 and O5, 2X zones, since his man has gone away from the ball. He should stand by the

free-throw line until O5 comes up. As soon as O5 delivers the
ball back to his man, he will move over to take him man-to-man,

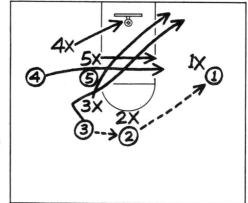

Diagram 89

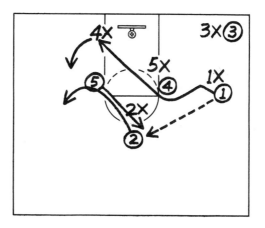

Diagram 90

since that side becomes the strong side. The frontline man who
is zoning that area will entertain him until 2X gets there. (See
Diagram 90.)

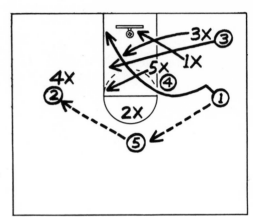

Diagram 91

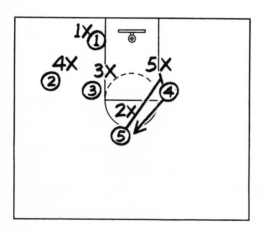

Diagram 92

O3's defender (3X) starts to zone as soon as the ball is thrown back to O2, and zones until his man goes into the post as the second cutter. (See Diagram 91.)

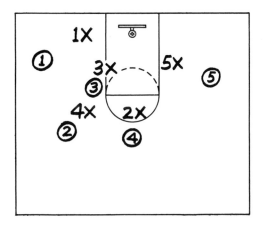

Diagram 93

At the moment O2 reaches the head of the circle, the zoning baseline (1X) man on that side must cover the goal cut by O1 and the middle man (4X) in the baseline zone must momentarily cover the man at the head of the circle (See Diagram 92.) Diagram 93 shows the defensive position of all men after two complete turn-overs of the shuffle.

Obviously, some offensive players have opportunities to take free-lance moves and would hurt you if they did. Your stunting defense in this case is predicated on the assumption that the team is so set they will not take openings they are not accustomed to getting and will be confused when their normal shots do not develop.

The California Pattern

The strong-side defense will be even more effective in defensing the California pattern, since normally a forward never comes up to the head of the circle.

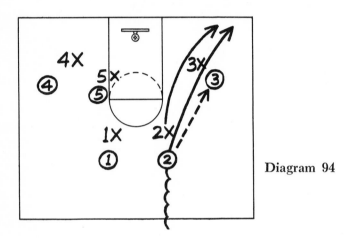

Diagram 94

As the ball is moved into initial position, the off-side guard is sloughing, since his man is on the weak side, as in Diagram 94.

On the penetration, the passing guard goes through, and since his man is going to the strong side, his defender will go with him man-to-man. The weak-side guard sloughs and watches his man. When his man moves to the point, he picks him up man-to-man and plays him through man-to-man while he goes through to the corner. (See Diagram 95.)

The baseline men zone and the other guard zones until his man goes to the point. (See Diagram 96.)

This action is repeated if the normal California pattern is followed.

The corner option would be nullified because the baseline

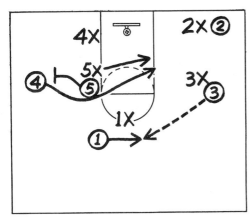

Diagram 95

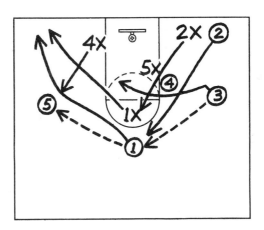

Diagram 96

men are zoning. To use this counter-move, the forward passes
to the corner man, who, being a guard, is defended man-to-man.
The passer moves in to the side post, offering a moving screen
to the side post man, who rolls out and around. Since both
defenders are zoning, a stalemate results. (See Diagram 97.)

To use the strong-side defense most effectively, two fast,
aggressive, harassing guards are helpful. A team with a relatively
slow frontline and fast guards could present a lot of trouble for
its opponents with the strong-side defense.

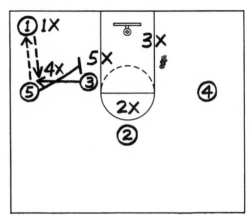

Diagram 97

It would surely change the rhythm of a game. If your opponents were moving smoothly and getting their shots, this defense
would bring an immediate change in the tempo of the game.
Teams that adjust poorly to different defenses would be at a
disadvantage.

This defense could be concealed very well. One way to do
this would be to have your guards press fullcourt, hurrying the
opposition down floor and into their offense with no oppor-

tunity to define the defense. If they normally like to play slowly, you have gained one advantage already by speeding up the tempo of their game. The baseline men should match up and appear to be playing man-to-man. After the guards penetrate the scoring area, the rules for strong-side combination defense should be applied. It might take some time for the offense to catch on, and even if they can identify the defense, the job of attacking it is no easy matter.

9

Scouting

Most people fear the unknown. Scouting reports are designed to eliminate this fear. They help to produce a logical plan of attack against opposing teams. The coach who can accurately evaluate information about his opponents will add many points throughout the course of the season, as well as reduce his opponent's scores.

Scouting is absolutely necessary today, if you plan to stunt defenses. There might be a few instances when a stunting defense could be used against a team that has not been scouted, but this is highly inadvisable.

PROFESSIONAL PREPARATION

Scouting is one of the best learning devices. Not only are you learning something about the team you are preparing to play, but you are also improving yourself professionally, since you are looking at the game from an analytical standpoint. In studying the strategy, the offensive and defensive patterns, and the individual players, you will gain insight into some of your own mistakes as well. In addition, the team you are scouting might use a pattern or some other idea that you may want to incorporate into your own style of play.

THE SCOUT

Some coaching staffs do not have enough coaches to secure the information needed in preparing a defense for a future game. Smaller high schools, especially, are faced with this problem. However, there are ways of overcoming this shortage of manpower and these ought to be looked into before definite commitments on stunting defenses are made.

Former players, faculty members, and other school friends may well serve as adequate scouts when there are no members of the coaching staff available. Newspaper reports and statistics could provide some information, although these are not the most reliable. The main thing is to obtain an unprejudiced, objective report on the over-all strength of your opponent. It is a great help if your scout thoroughly understands your own system. His analysis of the opposing team's strengths and weaknesses must be made in light of your strengths and weaknesses.

The trend in recent years has been to emphasize the importance of securing scout reports. To go into a game on even terms, the coach must obtain some type of first-hand information on the opposing team, since the vast majority of teams regularly scout their opponents. Scouting is as essential to pregame preparation in basketball as it is in any other sport. Those who do not scout operate at a definite disadvantage.

CHARTS

The clipboard is the scout's best friend, since few people have memories good enough to remember the many little intricacies that occur in a basketball game. A scout should have something to write on, and a written report should be required.

Different types of charts are available for scouting purposes. These can be bought commercially or can be devised by a coach to suit his own needs.

Usually, shot charts are more important to defensive preparation. By looking at the shot chart, a coach can learn a number of things. First, shot charts reveal which player takes the most shots and who the best percentage shooter is. (See Diagram 98.) On the basis of this information, it is easy to see who must be closely guarded and who can be sloughed on.

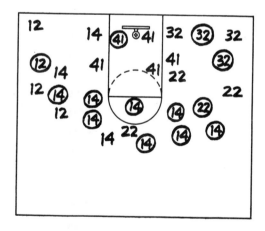

Diagram 98

Second, shot charts point out the area of the floor from which a team shoots the most. For instance, a shot chart showing good outside shooting would be a warning against using a zone. (See Diagram 99.)

Also, many teams take the majority of their shots from one side of the floor. Since most players are righthanded and would rather go right, the majority of shots in a game are usually made from the right side of the floor. Knowing this, a coach can

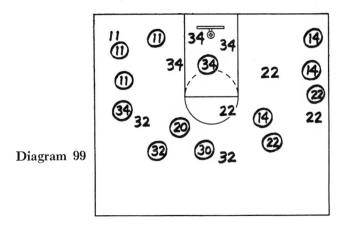

Diagram 99

make some adjustment that will strengthen the defense on the right side. It should impress on your players that they must overplay and force the defense to the left. (See Diagram 100.)

Ball-handling and rebounding charts can also be valuable assets in building your game tactics. Be careful to have your scout chart only those things he understands completely. Too much information, or information compiled erroneously, can be detrimental.

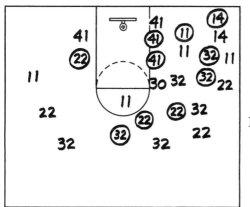

Diagram 100

EIGHT VITAL QUESTIONS

There are certain offensive maneuvers and team characteristics which it is essential to know in compiling a top-notch scout report. Knowledge of your opponent's offensive. attack will strengthen your chances of victory. No defensive attack can be consistently successful without some knowledge of the opponent's offensive plans.

In preparing a defense for an upcoming game, answers to the following eight vital questions are a must:

1. Do the opponents fast-break? If so, when—rebound situations, jumps balls, free throws, out of bounds, interceptions?
2. Do the opponents run a set or free-lance offense?
3. Do they cue patterns with hand signals, vocal signals, or by using some other method?

4. How do they initiate their offense? (Many offenses are
   started with an initial pass to the forward—examples:
   Drake Shuffle, Wheel, Kentucky Guard Series.)
5. What are the counter-moves when passes and cuts are
   overplayed?
6. What is the basic floor balance?
7. Do they work the pivot—can he go both ways?
8. How do they react to halfcourt and fullcourt pressure?
   Who are their poorest ballhandlers?

Of course, in answering these questions, any additional comments and diagrams will enhance the value of the scouting
report. Additionally, a brief sketch of opposing players will
be of invaluable assistance in determining the type of defense
to be used.

PLAYER SKETCHES

The individual player sketches should include the player's
number, name, height, weight, and position. Noticeable physical
features such as color of hair, knee supporters, or any peculiar
mannerisms a boy has should be included. The scout is trying
to familiarize his players with the personnel of another team.
Chances are these players are total strangers to them, so every
bit of information will help them to form a mental picture of
their opponents.

Be sure to include in the scout report which is the strong
hand of each player. Knowing whether a player is left-handed
or right-handed is a tremendous asset in preparing defense and
setting up assignments.

On the other hand, be careful to note which players can use
either hand effectively. Although most prefer to go one way,

occasionally there will be a ball player who can go both ways equally well. These players cannot be overplayed as effectively.

In scouting, one should be careful to note the temperament and attitude of each individual ball-player. Likewise, team unity and cohesiveness are noticeable features to which the scout should pay special attention. These intangible characteristics are often more important in winning a game than the more standard information garnered from a scout report.

How a player reacts after a mistake, or his reaction to an official's call, can change the direction of a game in a matter of seconds. A player who becomes irritated at an official's call may be so disgusted that he commits another infraction very soon. Some players are not able to overcome mistakes. They seem to bog down after one mistake and commit a series of them thereafter.

PHYSICAL FEATURES OF PLAYING AREA

If the game is to be played away from home, the physical environment of the playing area should be scouted. The size and type of court should influence the decision concerning the type of defense you will play. Generally, zones are more effective on smaller courts. The location of the players' bench might affect your decision to use signals in game. The crowd reaction will also influence the type of signals, verbal or visual, to be used.

Other information—pertaining to the type of backboards, ball, and officials—should be included. These could well have a psychological effect on the performance of your team.

PREPARING THE SCOUT REPORT

When all of this information has been gathered, organize it and present it to the players in written form. Go over the scouting report in a skull session, giving each player the opportunity to make comments and ask questions. Have each player file his report for future reference and set up in your own office a file for scout reports.

We like to begin each scout report with an aphorism or philosophical saying. A colorful remark at the start of the report tends to give the players a certain feeling of positiveness. It causes them to look forward to each report. One of the aphorisms that has created interest for us has been, "It's not how tall you are, but how tall you play." After a close defeat, the aphorism on the next scout report might read, "Our greatest glory is not in never failing, but in rising every time we fall." Over the years, we have accumulated a number of these short, philosophical statements that we use for various purposes.

Make the scout report interesting as well as challenging. Use every ounce of creative ability you possess to draw special attention to the more important features of the report.

At the end of the report, include a brief summary. It is wise to include in this summary an enumerated list of the things that must be done to insure victory. After the game, you will be able to look over that brief list and most likely be able to single out the items accounting for your team's failure or success on that particular night. Be specific. Give the players a goal to work for.

I well remember an outstanding defensive performance turned in by my first high school team. We were to face a neighboring rival in the first game of the regional tournament. In the last game of the preceding season, we had been beaten by this same team.

Our defensive goal was to hold the opponent to 20 points. Since the players were to do the defending, I allowed them to set the goal. They felt the figure 20 represented a realistic total. At half-time, the score was 23-20, our favor. After a few pointed remarks at half-time, we returned and held the opponents scoreless for a quarter-and-a-half. In the latter part of the game, as we emptied the bench, the opponents scored one field goal and one free throw, for a total of 23 points for the night.

CHOOSING THE DEFENSE

Once the coach has made an exhaustive study of the scout report, he is ready to decide what type of defense he will use. In making this decision, keep in mind the specific advantages of stunting defenses as set forth in Chapter 1. Never decide on a defense until the scout report has been thoroughly reviewed.

At this point, it is easy to overcoach. Do not stunt just for the sake of showing off your coaching ability. Have some justifiable reason for selecting a particular defense.

There are some general rules that can be of assistance in determining the type of defense to be used. For example, combination and pressure defenses are *usually* more effective against pattern teams, and alternating defenses *generally* work well against free-lance teams. Also, the size of the playing area and the individual ability of each player must be thoroughly considered.

OTHER FEATURES OF THE SCOUT REPORT

In addition, a good scout report will include a run-down on the various defenses used by your upcoming opponent. Make sure your team knows how to attack the different defenses you anticipate. Do not be defeated by a pressure defense because your team has failed to practice against it.

Jump-ball lineups and free-throw alignments should complement the scout report. Tactical maneuvers such as stall offenses and last-shot plays can win close games if you are prepared to defend them.

The following is a sample scout report as compiled during a recent season:

DOKES COLLEGE SCOUT REPORT

"Half-measures and half-desires indicate only half-men."

Personnel

Bob Smith, #40—right forward, 6'4", strong, blond-headed boy. Weighs about 190 or 195 lbs. Very aggressive ball player who will team with their pivot man to make a tough rebounding pair. He shoots the jump shot real well. Right-hander.

Sam Garner, #32—left forward, 6'4", not as strong looking as the other forward. He is not real thin, either. He wears glasses and even though he is pretty well put together, he did not get under the boards nearly as much as the pivot man and the other forward. He is the best 6'4" jump shooter I have seen this year. He takes a good on balance jump shot, and makes it. Has a real good touch. Likes to drive toward the baseline from the left forward spot and jump from about 20 or 25 feet. Right-handed.

Bob Davis, #50. This 6'5" hatchet man is averaging four tip-ins per game. He keeps a poker face (doesn't change expressions the whole game) and commits mayhem all the time. If the referee calls a foul, he doesn't say anything or do anything but lines up for the free throw; he just goes right back to committing murder again. Likes to work on the left side of the key on the side, get the ball from the left forward and slide under with one dribble for a jump lay-up. He wants *inside*. He will not hurt us if we can keep him outside on offense or defense. He wants *close* to that goal. He is real strong and knows it. If he gets the ball in close he is hard to stop. I am sure he wants to get in there real close to basket. He has dirty, sandy hair with what looks like a mohawk crew haircut.

He has a heavy beard and a hatchet face. Weighs about 200 pounds and is well put together. Left-hander.

Joe Russell, #10—guard, thin, small "blue darter", who never idles his engine. They fast-break and he is the fast part of their break. In all truth, though: their big men get downcourt real well and even run the middle (dribbling) lane on the break quite often. Russell is fast and quite aggressive on defense. He overcommits a lot trying to intercept and gambles too much. I think the man he is guarding must be alert but can take advantage of his foolish attempts to intercept passes. The passer must be alert when throwing to the man being guarded by him because he is fast and will get some of them. He is an unusually outstanding *ball-handler* and *dribbler*. Right-handed but uses left well.

Van Simpson, #34—guard, very dark haired boy about 6'. He is bigger and stronger looking than Russell. He has the long jump shot and drives real well to his left, even though he is right-handed. He is a fine basketball player but not as dangerous as Russell. Right-handed.

Don Miller, #14—6'2", senior. Played junior college ball before coming to Dokes. He is left-handed and a fine long shooter with the flat-footed one-hander. In addition, he has a fine jump shot. He did not fight the boards hard the night I saw him. He has a thin face and stoop shoulders.

DOKES COLLEGE OFFENSE

This will be the smartest team we play. Actually, I guess we would have to rank them along with State with regard to team strength, team organization, team pattern, shooting, smartness, and the total game. I fear that coaching is overrated in a lot of instances and I usually do not refer to their coaching when writing scout reports on an opponent. However, in this case, I was quite impressed. This young man knows what he is doing. His players know what he wants and they are sold on doing it just exactly right every time. We have been scouted only a few times by teams who live that far from us.

FIRST AND BASIC OPTION

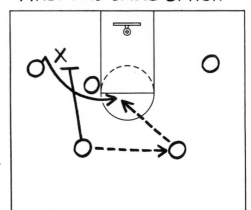

Diagram 101

2ND OPTION-CONTINUATION OF 1ST

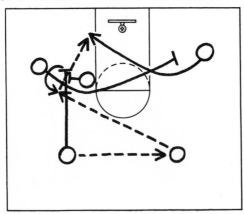

Diagram 102

They *fast-break*. It will be the best fast-break we'll see. I guess we will have to wait and determine whether their break is better than State's, for both of them fast-break

3RD OPTION—CONTINUATION OF INITIAL PLAY

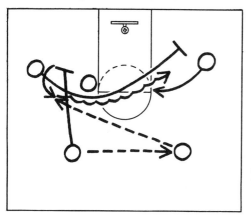

Diagram 103

4TH OPTION OFF SAME MANEUVER

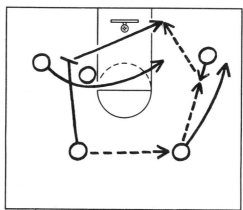

Diagram 104

beautifully. They get the *big men* in on the break better
than anyone we have ever played. That means we all have
to run back on defense.

5TH OPTION

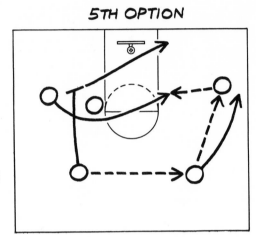

Diagram 105

They run this give-and-go several times each
game. I don't see how it fits into their pattern. Looks too easy but it worked.

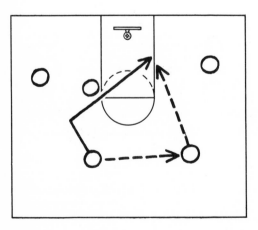

Diagram 106

Note: Options #4 and #5 look precisely like the total Western offense. They mix those two very good maneuvers with some stuff that is much better. Remember that all of this can be run to the right side of the floor, too.

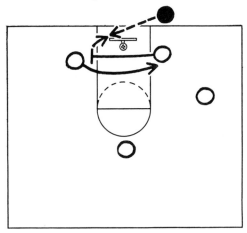

Diagram 107

They run a good *offensive pattern.* I am more impressed with the versatility of their offense and its uniqueness than any I've seen. I believe it is strictly theirs, for I have never seen it before. The basic principle they operate from on offense is the pass and screen *opposite.* They get many options and continuity off this principle.

The pattern is usually initiated by the left guard. He will hit the right guard with a pass and screen opposite for a series of moves.

DOKES DEFENSE

They used a rather tight halfcourt pressure type man-to-man against Howard. They alternated this basic defense of pressure with a deep sag, picking up the guards at the head of the circle. They mixed these two methods up quite a bit in an effort to confuse the opposing guards bringing the ball into play.

They will switch only when forced to. I counted only four switches all night when they played Howard. Part

of the game they pressed fullcourt man-to-man. A local
high school coach told me that they had used a zone press

POST FEED - STRAIGHT

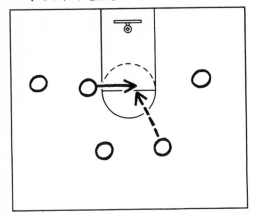

Diagram 108

POST FEED — SIDE

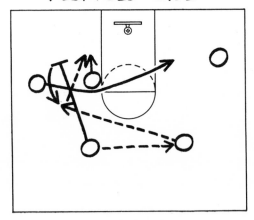

Diagram 109

fullcourt and also a halfcourt regular 2-1-2 defense. Since they scouted us, I imagine they will do everything they can to get us out of our pattern. Probably use a halfcourt zone and a fullcourt press and a halfcourt press.

They play on their own court and it is 94 by 50, with transparent boards. There is not enough room under one

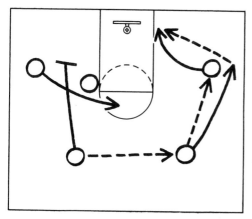

Diagram 110

goal but it is not a poor playing environment at all. The officials come from the Metro Conference, which is a very fine conference. This means that we should get impartial treatment from them. They will not be from Dokes.

10

Defensive Gimmicks

Human beings are endowed with a distinct characteristic: they would rather attack than defend. Basketball players are not exempt from this trait. Even coaches get trapped by the pleasures of offense. Human nature has provided us with an instinct that makes us want to be on the offensive. Society reinforces that instinct. Those who attack the best reap the rewards. Few basketball players make All-Americans on their ability to defend.

Young players begin developing their offensive skills while they are still in elementary school. Yet many of these same players never receive fundamental defensive instruction until they reach college. Offense is as natural as teen-age romance. Defense is unnatural; it is bothersome.

There has been little motivation for a player to concentrate on defense. Coaches have devised every conceivable method to improve offensive skills. Shooting rings that make the basket smaller, tipping apparatus, heavy and no-bounce basketballs, and dribble glasses have all been used to stimulate and motivate players to greater offensive achievements. In the past few years, there have been developed a number of defensive teaching aids that motivate interest in defense.

Teaching defensive basketball requires a great deal of effort and imaginative thinking. The players must be motivated. A coach can expound on defense until he is blue in the face, but if defense is not interesting and challenging to the players, maximum results will never be achieved. Most players will readily admit the importance of defense to their season's record, but they also tend to rely on the other players to carry the defensive load. Defense should be a positive factor.

A freshman walked onto the Oglethorpe campus just as the small liberal arts school was coming to be recognized as a small college basketball power. Since word was soon spread that the gangling youngster was a basketball player, various inquiries were made by students as to the position he played.

"Shooter," was his boastful reply.

Quite often, such an attitude is the rule rather than the exception. Box scores do not reveal the difference in points scored by two players. Newspaper headlines almost always praise the 20-point man. They seldom point out how many points the man he was guarding scored.

Defense is not a magic word. It does not come simply because the coach wants his team to be a good defensive club. Good defense requires hard work and imaginative thinking on the part of both the coach and players. Good defensive ball clubs are developed over a long period of time. Defense becomes a way of life not only to the coach, but to the players themselves. Pride must be developed in the fact that other teams have a difficult time scoring.

Successful defensive coaches are those who can sell defense

and make it attractive. Defensive teaching aids are a great help in this direction. They not only improve team and individual skills, but they also make the defensive practice more enjoyable. Team morale is improved considerably by the use of these teaching aids.

WEIGHT TRAINING

Defense requires strength. A good defensive player must be able to absorb the bumps and bruises to which he will be exposed. Contact is becoming more and more a part of basketball. Basketball players are getting bigger and stronger, so it is important that muscles are developed to withstand the punishment.

Since defense is played in an unnatural position—boxer's stance—strength and the development of back and leg muscles should be a part of the over-all development program. There are a number of "gimmicks" and weight-training apparatus that can be used to achieve this goal.

Weight training has been one of the most popular ways of adding extra bulk and strength. According to Delorme's principles of resistive exercise, weak muscles should be subjected to strenuous exercise at regular intervals to the point of maximum exertion. Since basketball is a game that does not produce focal muscle development, out-of-season weight programs will help to strengthen your basketball program. Most of the best defensive players are strong, well-conditioned athletes.

There are probably as many different weight-training programs as there are teams that use them. In searching for a suitable group of exercises, the amount of time available for weight work is a strong determining factor. Players will lose interest if the weight workout is prolonged.

The following exercises meet the needs of the average basket-ball player. Others may be added if the boy is extremely thin or overweight. The starting weights [1] are indicated in the parentheses:

Overhead press ($\frac{1}{3}$ body weight plus 10)
Bench press ($\frac{1}{2}$ body weight)
Arm curls ($\frac{1}{3}$ body weight plus 10)
Squats ($\frac{1}{2}$ body weight plus 10)
Heel raises ($\frac{1}{2}$ body weight plus 10)
Sit ups (No weight)

The best way to implement this program is to divide the team into groups according to their relative body sizes and strength. About three players per bar will keep the lifting period to a minimum length of time. Have each player complete the first series of lifting exercises by using the designated starting weights. Ten repetitions compose the first set.

The second set should be done with an additional 10 pounds per lift, and the repetitions reduced to 8. The third set will have another 10 pounds added, and the repetitions further reduced to 6.

When a player can perform each exercise through 10 repetitions at each weight, then it is time to up his starting weight. Add 10 pounds and repeat the cycle as explained above.

For example, a boy who weighs 150 pounds would start at 60 pounds for the overhead press. When he can lift 60 pounds 10 times, 70 pounds 10 times, and 80 pounds 10 times, he will move his starting weight to 70 pounds. At the starting weight of 70 pounds, the first set would include 10 repetitions, the second set 8 repetitions, and the third 6 repetitions.

---

[1] Gene Hooks, *Application of Weight Training to Athletics* (Englewood Cliffs, N.J., Prentice-Hall, Inc., 1960), p. 42.

A weight rack will produce stronger legs. The rack will enable players to use more weight for the heel-raise and three-quarter squats.

Supervision of the weight program by the coach is necessary to its over-all success. Few athletes will follow a prescribed lifting pattern unless there is someone in a supervisory capacity. Also, there may be a tendency for some athletes to go overboard in the development of the muscles in one particular part of the body. One may be interested only in the leg muscles, while another might concentrate completely on the muscles in the upper extremities.

Defense requires well-developed muscles in all parts of the body. A well-supervised and continuous weight-training program will condition the athlete for the rigors of a tough defensive game. The carry-over to other parts of the game is invaluable.

WEIGHTED SHOES, ANKLE-WEIGHTS, GALOSHES

A number of successful coaches have in the past few years added weight to the footwear of their players to emphasize defensive footwork. These extra weights are worn during the defensive portion of their workout and on some occasions throughout the entire practice session.

The weighted basketball shoe is one of the most popular innovations, because it is comfortable to the player. It requires no bothersome effort to wear and can be worn just like an ordinary basketball shoe. Produced by a nationally prominent company the weighted shoe has weight graduated throughout the sole of the shoe.

Ankle-weights have been devised to accomplish the same purpose as the weighted shoe. They can be strapped around the ankle quickly. Little time is needed to adjust them. These, too, are produced commercially; and varying amounts of weights can be obtained, depending on the leg strength of the player using them.

Neal Baisi at West Virginia Tech popularized the use of rubber galoshes as a leg conditioner during his defensive practices. The boot-type rubber galoshes can be quickly fitted over the basketball shoe, since there is no need to worry about blisters.

All of these weights are designed to overload the leg muscles and are appropriate for almost all defensive drills. When the weights are removed, the players will find their speed and quickness have increased.

Some coaches like to send their teams through a rigid conditioning program in the fall. They take advantage of the warm weather and have their players run cross-country. This is an ideal time to make use of the ankle-weights and weighted shoes. Running stadium steps will help to build up the leg muscles even more.

The football field can be used as a conditioning area. Pressing defenses can be practiced there while the players wear weight on their feet. Practicing the press on the football field will certainly make that 94 x 50 area appear to be much smaller.

DEFENSIVE HARNESS

One of the most ingenious devices for teaching defense was developed by Elmer Morrow, formerly head basketball coach at Druid Hills High School, and presently Director of Athletics, DeKalb County Schools, Decatur, Georgia. The defensive harness is made from dog collars and is designed to keep the defensive player in a low crouch. Maintaining a good defensive stance

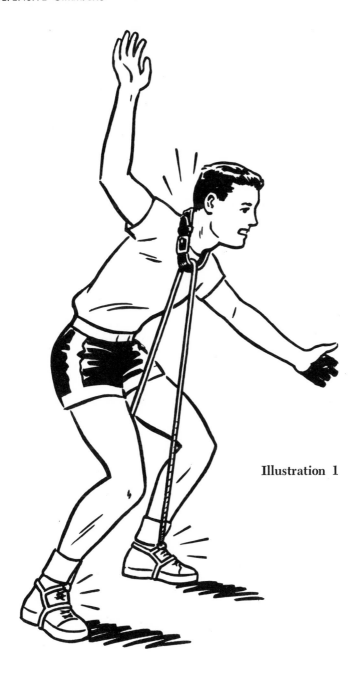

Illustration 1

is important to every defense, no matter how conventional or unorthodox the defense is.

The harness is not produced on a commercial basis, but can be easily made. One dog collar is placed around the neck. This collar consists of a single piece of leather about one inch wide. Two more dog collars are worn on each foot. These are the type collars the dog wears on his back. A rope is extended from one foot, through the collar on the neck, to the other foot. Since the rope is adjustable, it can be shortened to keep the player as low as the coach wants.

There is no danger of injury from the use of the defensive harness. Complete freedom of movement is allowed, but of course it is impossible for the defensive player to raise up. The player wearing the harness must stay low and slide his feet by using the boxer's shuffle rather than crossing them.

The harness can be used while practicing individual defensive skills or during team drills. Every move on defense can be executed while wearing the harness except rebounding. Players can block-out for the rebound but cannot jump to retrieve the ball.

Using the harness is a good way of emphasizing the importance of the block-out in defensive rebounding. Have the players form a rebounding cup around the basket when they block-out and let the rebound fall to the floor. They will easily see that no matter how high they can jump, position will usually determine the number of rebounds they get in game situations.

REBOUNDING MACHINES

A number of attempts have been made to construct rebounding devices. Most of them have been cumbersome pieces of equipment which would not stand up to the abuses of defensive rebounding. Since the ball must be jerked away from opposing offensive players, we have found the rebounding machine developed by Fred McCall, head basketball coach at Campbell College, to be an effective piece of equipment in teaching defensive rebounding.

The rebounder is built in such a way that players are forced to rebound with two hands. The rebounder consists of a basket with an arm extending from the basket. The basket is attached to an adjustable base and can be raised up or down according to a player's height and jumping ability. A spring or hydraulic press makes a strong pull necessary to remove the ball from its resting position.

Individual rebounding skills are best taught on this machine. The one-on-one block-out and the actual grasping of the ball can be practiced. The rebounder also serves as an incentive for boys to increase their jumping ability, since the height at which the ball is taken off the machine is indicated on the adjustable base.

Practicing the defensive block-out on a team basis has always presented a problem to coaches. If a five-on-five drill, with the defensive team blocking out the offensive team, is used, the coach has to concentrate on missing the basket so that the rebound will come off at the correct angle. He cannot look to check the block-out technique being used by the players.

An electrical device has been perfected to solve this problem. It fits inside the basket, is attached to the rim, and kicks the ball out in the same manner that a rebound would come off the rim. The ball comes off at a different angle each time. This gimmick is perfect for practicing defensive rebounding and the block-out, since it kicks the ball out of the basket at a rebounding angle every time.

Illustration 2

GLOVES

A relatively new innovation in defensive teaching aids, one that is especially useful in teaching zone defenses, is the use of gloves. This idea was conceived by Billy Carter, assistant basketball coach Oglethorpe University.

The first instruction a coach gives his team when playing a zone defense is to "keep your arms up." This simple practice increases the effectiveness of the zone defense at least 25 per cent. The use of bright-colored gloves will impress on your players the importance of keeping their arms extended.

This is a task that becomes laborious when the players get tired. Dropping the arms is one of the first signs of fatigue. It may be wise to keep their arms raised and have them wear the gloves while practicing the zone. Follow up this practice by making these players do some push-ups or other exercises to strengthen their arms after practice.

Show your team the value of keeping the arms raised. Line them up in the zone and ask them to raise their arms. The zone will look more compact and there will be few areas that look large enough to pass through. Point out the advantages, then ask them to drop their arms by their side. The critical scoring area covered so well with the arms extended will be practically bare.

HANDS BEHIND THE BACK

While it is important to keep the hands raised on the zone defense, some players have a tendency to depend too much on their hands for defensive purposes. They refuse to move their feet in order to keep their body in good defensive position. Instead, they like to slap, hook, and commit needless fouls.

If you are plagued with this sort of problem, conduct your defensive drills by having the players keep their hands behind their back. One-on-one, two-on-two, and even five-on-five drills are made more meaningful by emphasizing good footwork and body position instead of useless hacking and hooking.

CHAIRS

Coaches are always looking for some way to improve their teaching techniques. Sometimes, the best teaching aids are the most obvious. We occasionally stumble all around helpful teaching aids because we feel they might simplify things too much. Simplicity is the objective of every teaching aid. Never take anything for granted. Communication often breaks down between player and coach. Time out for a simple demonstration might save valuable points at game time.

One obvious teaching device is the folding chair. Usually, it is a nuisance. If too many of them are in the gym, the chairs attract uninvited guests to practice sessions. They might even encourage players to sit and take a brief respite before or after practice when they should be working. The coach might be lured into sitting position while practice is in progress. To avoid such situations, keep a few folding chairs in the gym, but store them out of sight, preferably in a place to which there will be easy access.

The part method is an extremely good way to teach defense. It brings good results because it allows the individual to concentrate on one aspect of the defense at a time. Before breaking down the defense into its different parts, show the complete defense to the squad before the actual practice of the defense is begun. The players will gain a better understanding of how the defense should function. They will know why they are performing certain drills.

Chairs can be used to represent defensive men. Gather the players in the bleachers to give them a high vantage point. Show the different defensive positions of each player by moving the chairs around on the floor. The players can get a good over-all idea of the relationship between their individual positions and a teammate's position.

Of course, the same objective can be accomplished by using the blackboard in a skull session. But by using folding chairs on the floor instead of X's on the blackboard, the players get a truer perspective of their contribution to the over-all success of the defense.

11

Teaching Stunting Defenses

Teaching defense in basketball involves an extremely hazardous obstacle. In athletics, those who are successful are able to surmount the psychological barrier and extend themselves to their physiological limits. The distance runner about to break a record reaches a point where he almost breaks his stride and begins to coast. However, because of previous conditioning he is able to overcome this urge and extend his pace for a while longer.

Successful athletes eliminate this psychological barrier. They do not quit when fatigue sets in. They know their bodies can take punishment far exceeding the limits they have experienced.

CHIEF PROBLEM IN COACHING DEFENSE

Basketball coaches face a problem similar to that of the mile runner. As the mile runner goes into his last lap, knowing he has a chance for the record, he has to decide whether or not he will kick a little harder or give in to his mental urgings and take it easy.

We like to compare basketball to the mile run. Offense is the first part of the run where everybody keeps pace. Defense is the last lap, the home stretch, where the champions are crowned. Every basketball player is more than willing to run the first part of the race. Few break through the psychological barrier and develop their defensive ability on their own. They do not want to run the complete race.

As a coach, it is your job to eliminate this psychological barrier and make defense interesting and challenging to your squad. When lactic acid begins to erase the irritability of the muscle fibers and fatigue creeps in, only the athlete who has experienced many hours of defensive drilling will be able to push himself to his physiological extent.

Reward the Best Defensive Player

Psychologists teach that positive reinforcements are more apt to produce favorable responses. Adopt this idea in your defensive approach. Make defense challenging, interesting, and pleasurable. Of course, the ultimate aim of a hard-nosed defense is victory. This in itself will not always motivate players to their maximum defensive efforts. Other incentives are needed.

Honor the best defensive player with a trophy each year. Let the squad members determine the recipient by casting their votes. Players can usually pick the defensive stand-outs more easily than the coaching staff, since they knock heads with each other every day.

Make sure newspaper writers recognize outstanding defensive efforts—both team and individual. Building a defensive *esprit de corps* among team members will make your job of teaching much easier.

Teaching Defense Is a Test of Coaching Ability

In no other phase of the game is the coach's ability to teach as evident as in his defensive preparation. Successful use of any of the defenses described in this book begin with the coach. Long-range planning and careful organization will enable you to install a new defense at strategic times during the season.

SCHEDULING

Defensive preparation begins long before the season starts. The first step actually involves arranging your schedule. Tactical defensive maneuvers will be impossible unless games are spaced on the schedule. Give yourself enough preparation time, whenever possible. Conference rules and league play may forbid direct scheduling, but in most cases it will be possible to see that there is enough time between games.

Back-to-Back Friday and Saturday Night Games

High school coaches are plagued with the problem of playing back-to-back games on Friday and Saturday nights. School administrators are increasingly refusing to allow games to be played on nights preceding a school day. Such an arrangement makes it impossible to prepare effectively for both games. When faced with this problem, it is better to direct your attention to the Friday night game and use normal defenses for the Saturday night game. Saturday morning skull sessions or a brief dummy workout will help to correct Friday night mistakes and give you time to make some small adjustments in the defense for the Saturday night opponent.

Try to avoid scheduling games on successive nights. Take advantage of holidays, teacher work days, and other days when school is not in session. Schedule games preceding these days, so that you will not be presented with this problem every week.

Stay Away from 2 and 3 Game Road Trips

Some colleges try to schedule several games on a lengthy road trip. While this may be good for the budget, it does not always result in an impressive won-lost record. Seldom will you run across two teams that can be defensed in the same manner. Sometimes, a short blackboard session with your team may enable you to make sufficient preparation for your opponent. Other teams might require several days of defensive work before you can hope to stop their attack. Familiarity with an opposing team's style of play and some basic convictions about how to defend against this style should be primary considerations when making your schedule.

MASTER THE FUNDAMENTALS FIRST

In the six weeks of pre-season practice, stunting defenses should seldom be mentioned. The majority of the defensive work during this period is devoted to fundamental work on defense. At this time, it is impossible to determine which, if any, of the defenses will be used. Scouting reports dictate defensive changes.

The first four weeks of practice are taken up with the basic defensive maneuvers described in Chapter 2. Work hard on your man-for-man defense, sliding or switching. If you have decided to be a switching team, compile a list of two-on-two and three-on-three switching situations and work these into your practice schedule throughout this four-week period. Make sure every player knows when to switch and when to slide.

Spend a lot of time on situations involving screens. Teach

your players how to play each situation according to your own
feelings about switching and sliding. Our man-for-man defense
has held up well by switching on all offensive crosses involving

INSIDE DRIBBLE WEAVE SCREEN

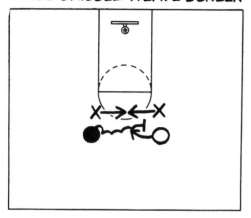

Diagram 111

SCREEN AND ROLL

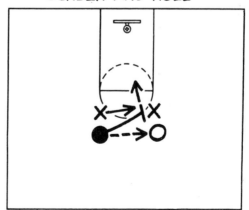

Diagram 112

the ball. By using the following break-down drills, players can learn to distinguish quickly between switching and non-switching situations. (See Diagrams 111-118.)

OUTSIDE DRIBBLE BLOCK SCREEN

Diagram 113

BLIND SCREEN

Diagram 114

SCREEN OPPOSITE

Diagram 115

GIVE-AND-GO

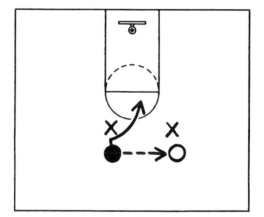

Diagram 116

A ball club that can handle all of these situations well will have a strong defense. Using the rule of switching on all crosses involving the ball, the first four diagrams represent switching situations, the last four sliding.

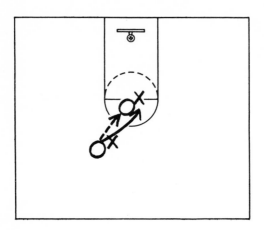

Diagram 117

In the fifth week, start to teach a zone defense. Teach only one zone defense, as we have already pointed out in Chapter 3. Flex the positions of each defensive player to match different offensive attack. From this same formation, develop your zone press attack. If you can go into the opening game of the season with a sound man-for-man defense and a zone defense of the same caliber, you will find as the season progresses a number of defensive weapons in your arsenal.

These two basic defenses may be enough to carry your team throughout the season. It may be possible that you will never have the occasion to alternate between the zone and man-for-man, to combine the two defenses, or to conceal either of the two. Nonetheless, there will be a larger number of defenses at your disposal.

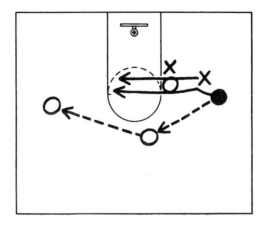

Diagram 118

TEACHING POINTERS

When the season starts and a decision is reached to use a stunting defense, have confidence in the defense you choose. Do not make the mistake of second-guessing once a decision on a defense has been made. Players react to game strategy more favorably when the coach's confidence is reflected through his actions.

Know the weaknesses and strengths of the defense. Try to anticipate rough spots and point them out to the players so they will be aware of the weaknesses. If they are alert to the weaknesses, then some compensation can be made to avoid being hurt in these areas.

Break down the defense and work on the component parts. If a zone and man-for-man alternation is planned, practice the zone and man-for-man separately before working on the cues that will make the alternation. A further break-down may be necessary. Drills designed to acquaint the defense with offensive patterns might be mandatory before the alternation will be effective.

If a combination zone-and-one defense is to be used, be sure to spend some time working on overplaying the superstars. Also, practice the other four men in the zone formation without the fifth defensive player. When the two parts of the defense are brought together, each player will understand his assignments better.

Give the defense an opportunity to jell. Patience is a necessity. A stunting defense will not be built in a day. The second day will show a definite improvement in the defense. A third, if available, will continue the progress. Do not hesitate to make adjustments where possible. Actual work on the court will most likely reveal some parts of the defense that need changing.

SKULL SESSION

The pre-game meeting is the last opportunity you, as the coach, will have to go over game strategy. Anything you might say in the dressing room before the game will probably be of little consequence if the players are keyed up and ready to go. Therefore, we have always deemed it necessary to meet several hours before game time and go over defensive strategy.

For the high school coach, the best time to get the players together for this meeting is immediately after school. The college coach will probably have to schedule his skull session around classes and labs. Before the pre-game meal is a good time to schedule the meeting. After the meal, players some-times get drowsy when they sit for any length of time.

Go over the scout report thoroughly, but be careful about prolonging the session. Have a general format organized so the meeting will not last more than 30 minutes. Review the player sketches and your offensive and defensive strategy. Ask specific questions of the players. Do everything in your power to erase doubt.

12

Drills

Basketball is a game of fundamentals. Intensive drilling develops the fundamental games until players blend together as a team. Athletic squads have been defined simply as a group of athletes with little teamwork. Athletic teams result from persistent drilling until the players have a sense of unity and familiarity with each other.

Drills should be designed to simulate game conditions as closely as possible. Do everything under pressure. Defense can be taught best at full speed. Dummy work does little more than acquaint the players with the way defense should be played. Defense is always full speed.

Use break-down drills to lead into team work. Try to gauge team work so that the players leave eager to defend a while longer. Keep the break-down drills as simple as possible. Do not spend too much time on one short-time drill during each prac-

187

tice. It is better to work a short time each day on one drill than to spend a long time on one drill for one day.

Keep the players active. Do not allow players to stand around and wait. Organize practice sessions so that each player is continually busy from the time practice starts until it ends. Whenever possible, divide the squad in two groups and have a group working on each end. It is best for this work to be supervised by a coach. However, if no assistant coach is available, a senior member of the team can sometimes provide leadership to conduct a drill at one end of the court while you are watching the other group.

Do not prolong the practice session unnecessarily. Go on the floor with a written practice schedule, with time allotments for each activity. Be prepared to organize drills and keep the players moving from one drill to another. Be specific in your directions.

Players who have real difficulty in performing a skill or executing a drill should be asked to stay after practice for special work. Do not penalize the entire squad if one member fails to pick up a desired skill that the other team members have learned.

In this chapter, you will see some of the drills that will contribute to complete mastery of defensive fundamentals, thereby laying the groundwork for later defensive stunts.

1. Sliding (Footwork Drill)

Procedure:

(a) Arrange squad on one half of the court as shown in diagram. Give each player plenty of room.

(b) The coach or manager can serve as leader. Dribble ball right, left, forward, and backward.

(c) The individual players should react as if they were

guarding the dribbler by moving from place to place through the use of the Boser's Shuffle.

Objectives:

(a) To teach body movement without crossing the feet.
(b) To encourage players to watch belt of offensive player.

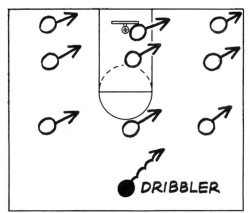

Diagram 119

(c) To condition back and leg muscles and the respiratory system for strenuous defensive play.
(d) To teach proper stance—one hand up to discourage shots, and one hand down to deflect passes and feel for screens.

2. Finding the Screen Drill

Procedure:

(a) Place 10 or more obstacles at random on the floor.

Chairs usually make good obstacles, although players can serve the same purpose.

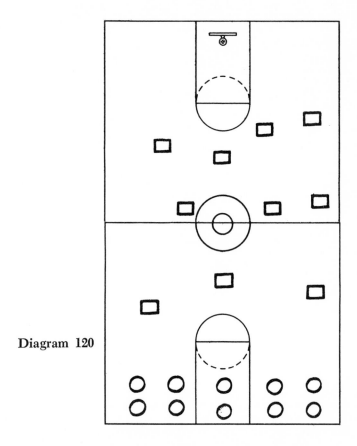

Diagram 120

(b) Arrange players in five lines at one end of floor.
(c) The first five men turn their backs to the opposite end of the floor and slide backward on coach's signal.

Objectives:

(a) Conditioning.

(b) Teaches players to feel for screens.

(c) Teaches defensive peripheral vision.

3. **Steal the Bacon**

Procedure:

(a) Arrange the squad along the baseline and divide them into two groups.

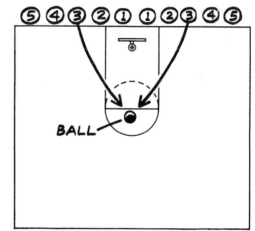

Diagram 121

(b) Place ball on free-throw line.

(c) Have each group count off until every player has a number.

(d) When the coach calls a number, the two players who havé been assigned the same number scramble for the ball.

The player getting possession of the ball is guarded by the other player in a one-on-one situation.

Objectives:

(a) Encourage aggressive retrieving of loose balls.
(b) Teach quick change-over to defense.
(c) Improve one-on-one defensive ability.

4. One-on-One Picking up the Dribbler

Procedure:

(a) Divide the squad into two groups—an offensive group and a defensive group—at opposite ends of the floor.

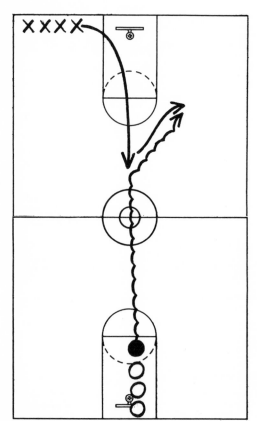

Diagram 122

(b) The first offensive player dribbles to the other end of the floor. He is picked up by the first defensive player, who guards him until the dribbler scores or loses possession of the ball.

(c) Players alternate lines.

Objectives:

(a) Develop one-on-one defensive ability.

(b) Force the dribbler to a halt before he reaches his position by faking and retreating.

5. Forcing Dribbler to Inside (One-on-One)

Procedure:

(a) Divide squad into two groups, one on each side of floor.

(b) Break each group into offensive and defensive lines.

(c) The first dribbler starts his move from the center side-line. The first defensive player moves out to guard the approaching offensive player.

(d) After each performance, the players change lines.

Diagram 123

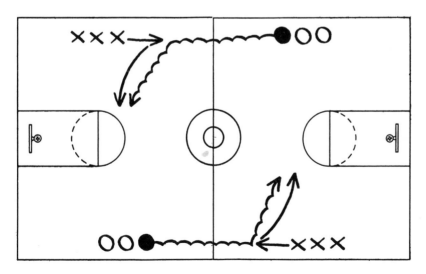

Objectives:

(a) Forces the dribbler to the inside.

(b) Cultivates good footwork, stance, and competitive defensive attitude.

6. Zone Breakdown Drill

Procedure:

(a) Arrange squad in semicircle as shown in diagram.

(b) Place three men on defense in 1-3-1 zone positions.

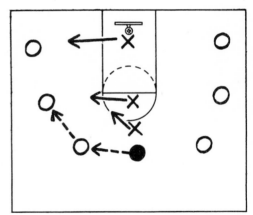

Diagram 124

(c) Players in semicircle move the ball. Each receiver holds the ball for a second after he catches it, then passes it to another player.

(d) Defensive players take normal 1-3-1 slides. Momentary pause after each pass will give defensive players opportunity to orient themselves.

(e) After three players have been on defense, they move to semicircle, and three offensive players go on defense until everyone has a turn.

Objectives:

(a) To teach slides of different zone positions.
(b) To eliminate doubt of defensive slides.

7. Baseline-Cutter Drill

Procedure:

(a) Arrange players in one line at a forward position.
(b) First man in line is first defensive player. After performance, players go from offense to defense to end of the line.
(c) Offensive player has two alternatives—pass and cut to ball or drive baseline.
(d) Defense should react accordingly.

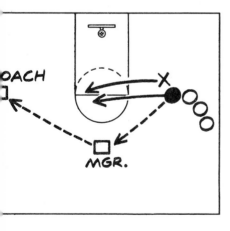 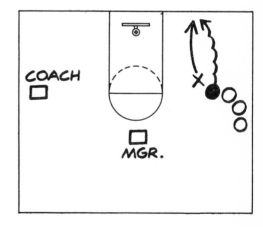

Diagram 125   Diagram 126

Objectives:

(a) Teach proper baseline play.

(b) Teach quick sag and overplay of cutters.

(c) Combines two important defensive maneuvers into one drill.

8. Rebound-Press Drill

Procedure:

(a) Pair team members according to speed and height.

(b) Toss the ball against the backboard. The two boys

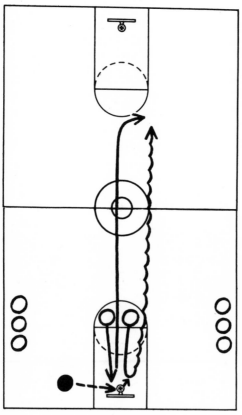

Diagram 127

waiting at the free-throw line go for the ball. The boy who gets the rebound becomes the offensive dribbler and the other becomes the presser.

(c) The dribbler tries to score at the other end of the floor.

(d) After each shot, the ball is free, whether it goes in or not. (These two players compete until one scores six points.)

Objectives:

(a) Develop aggressive one-on-one defensive block-out.

(b) Build stamina and endurance.

(c) Develop defensive pressing tactics.

9. Whistle Drill

Procedure:

(a) Arrange squad in a five-on-five halfcourt scrimmage situation with the first team on defense.

(b) Have the second team run your next opponent's offense.

(c) Instruct both teams to stop immediately upon hearing the sound of the whistle. Every player should remain in his position while listening to instructions of the coach.

(d) Blow whistle periodically and look for mistakes. Point these out and show correct floor position and coverage.

Objectives:

(a) Improve floor position on zone defenses.

(b) Emphasize importance of weak-side sag and overplay of cutters in man-for-man defense.

(c) Stress alertness on defense at all times.

10. Head-on Drill

Procedure:

(a) Divide the squad into two lines as shown in diagram.
(b) Instruct the dribbler to try to score by staying within the three-second lane extended.
(c) Have the defensive players step in front of the dribbler and draw the charging foul.
(d) Players change lines after each performance.

Objectives:

(a) Teaches defensive player to withstand contact and develops his courage.

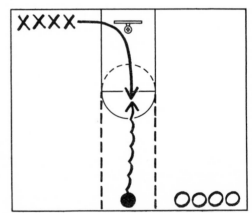

Diagram 128

(b) Prevents turning sideways and hooking dribbler.
(c) Encourages aggressive brand of defensive basketball.

These are some of the defensive drills we have found to be of tremendous value in developing sound defensive habits. Disciplined work in the fundamental areas of the defensive game will place at your disposal an unlimited number of defensive possibilities.

Index